READING THE THIRTIES

Critical Essays in Modern Literature

The Fiction and Criticism of Katherine Anne Porter (revised)
Harry L. Mooney, Jr.

Entrances to Dylan Thomas' Poetry
Ralph Maud

Joyce Cary: The Comedy of Freedom
Charles G. Hoffmann

The Short Stories of Ambrose Bierce
Stuart C. Woodruff

The Fiction of J. D. Salinger (revised)
Frederick L. Gwynn and Joseph L. Blotner

James Agee: Promise and Fulfillment
Kenneth Seib

Chronicles of Conscience: A Study of George Orwell and Arthur Koestler
Jenni Calder

Richard Wright: An Introduction to the Man and His Work
Russell Carl Brignano

Dylan Thomas' Early Prose: A Study in Creative Mythology
Annis Pratt

The Situation of the Novel
Bernard Bergonzi

D. H. Lawrence: Body of Darkness
R. E. Pritchard

The Hole in the Fabric: Science, Contemporary Literature, and Henry James
Strother B. Purdy

Reading the Thirties: Texts and Contexts
Bernard Bergonzi

READING THE THIRTIES
Texts and Contexts

Bernard Bergonzi

University of Pittsburgh Press

First published in Great Britain 1978 by
The Macmillan Press Ltd

Published in the U.S.A. by the
University of Pittsburgh Press

178632

Library of Congress Cataloging in Publication Data

Bergonzi, Bernard.
    Reading the thirties.

    1. English literature—20th century—History and criticism.   2. Litera-
ture and society.   3. England—Civilization—20th century.   I. Title.
PR471.B45   820'.9'00912   78-4262
ISBN 0-8229-1135-3

Printed in Great Britain by offset lithography by
Billing & Sons Ltd, Guildford, London and Worcester

FOR DAVID AND MARY LODGE

Contents

1937

For me it was a time of bandages
and so it was in Spain.
I heard there was a war in Spain:
I knew where Spain was on a map.

A further piece of surgery impended,
but in the end was not performed.
A further war impended too; I did not know.

And I knew nothing
of the bright-eyed poets in open shirts,
of the last mile to Huesca
and the Attlee Battalion;
of clean untrammelled function in life and art;
Ben Nicholson's squares and circles,
the Health Centre at Peckham;
Stalin's Five-Year Plan.

I had not sensed
the perilous freedom in the air beyond the pylons
eluding the ferrety pale cyclists.
I had not seen, O machine's-miracle-marvel,
a Bristol Bulldog loop the loop
high over Salisbury Plain.

But I devoured *Modern Wonder*
and several comics, weekly.
My bandages grew smaller,
Franco's troops moved north and east,
the Junkers pummelled free Madrid.

I was a child and sickly in those years.
But I have read the histories,
have learnt the things I was too young to know.
I feel my memories
crystallizing into myth.

Acknowledgements

My thanks are due to my wife and Bridgit O'Toole, who read parts of this book in manuscript; to Audrey Cooper, of the University of Warwick Library; to the editors of *Encounter*, where earlier versions of chapters 2 and 6 first appeared; and to the participants in an undergraduate seminar on the literature of the 1930s that I taught in 1975–76 and 1976–77.

The author and publishers wish to thank the following who have kindly given permission for the use of copyright material:

Professor Miriam Allott, for an extract from 'Signs', by Kenneth Allott, from *New Verse*.

Curtis Brown Limited, on behalf of Christopher Isherwood, for an extract from 'Lions and Shadows'.

Faber and Faber Limited, for extracts from 'A, a, a, Domine Deus', from *Sleeping Lord* by David Jones.

Faber and Faber Limited and Random House Inc., for extracts from 'Pylons' and 'The Express', from *Collected Poems* by Stephen Spender.

A. M. Heath & Company Limited, on behalf of Mrs Sonia Brownell Orwell, for an extract from 'On a Ruined Farm Near His Master's Voice Gramophone Factory', by George Orwell, published by Martin Secker & Warburg.

William Heinemann Limited, for a passage by Edward Upward, quoted in *Lions and Shadows* by Christopher Isherwood.

A. D. Peters Limited, on behalf of Mrs Day Lewis, for an extract from 'The Road These Times Must Take', by C. Day Lewis, from *Left Review—1934*.

Lawrence Pollinger Limited and The Viking Press Inc., for extracts from Graham Greene's novels, published by William Heinemann and The Bodley Head.

Random House Inc., for an extract from 'Essay on Rime' by Karl Shapiro.

Introduction

This book is not about all of the literature written in England between 1930 and 1940. In the title, and throughout the book, I use the term 'the thirties' in the same deliberately selective fashion that made it possible for Edward Upward to give the all-embracing title, *In the Thirties*, to a retrospective novel about the progress of a young poet and schoolmaster from bourgeois individualism to the Communist Party which restricted itself to a dozen or so characters. Despite this narrowness of range, Stephen Spender could still call Upward's novel 'the most truthful picture of life in that decade'. In the present book I do not intend 'the thirties' to mean just a period, but also to refer generically to a group of writers and the work they produced, mostly in that decade, occasionally later. Indeed, 'the thirties' in this sense largely corresponds to what Samuel Hynes, in his recent admirable study of literature and politics at that time, calls 'the Auden generation'. The thirties generation mythologised themselves as they lived and wrote, and I have long been fascinated by the mythology, as the preceding poem will indicate. It was written in 1963 and first published in 1967, in a slightly longer version, in the little magazine *Tracks*. I reprint it here, not out of any strong conviction of its literary merit, but because it briefly tries to capture, in imagery and language, characteristics that I discuss at greater length in this book. There is the foregrounding of lists and isolated typological images, with a stylistic tendency to strings of nominal phrases and an abundant use of definite articles. There is also a touch

of the Hopkinsese that young poets tried out in the early
thirties. (Some allusions may, with the passing of time,
need annotating: 'the last mile to Huesca' is from John
Cornford's poem 'Heart of the Heartless World'; the Attlee
Battalion was the British formation in the International
Brigades; and the Peckham Health Centre was a much-ad-
mired example of a neighbourhood welfare unit.) This poem
represents the remote genesis of the present book, and
shows that my interest in the thirties long antedates the
attention that began to be directed at the period from
about 1975 onwards. This new interest was evident in
the 'Young Writers of the Thirties' exhibition at the National
Portrait Gallery, London, in the summer of 1976, and
in such books as A. T. Tolley's *The Poetry of the Thirties*,
Samuel Hynes's *The Auden Generation*, the new edition of
Julian Symons's *The Thirties: A Dream Revolved*, and Christopher Isherwood's autobiographical *Christopher and His Kind*.
Parts of the present work were written, or drafted, before
these books appeared; in other parts I am indebted to
them, though my approach to the literary history of the
thirties is rather different from theirs.

My interest is less in extendedly discussing individual
authors, or individual texts, than in trying to read the
thirties as a collective subject, even a collective text. The
approach involves certain departures from the familiar
methods and assumptions of English criticism, and not all
of this book can be called literary criticism, though all
of it stays close to literary texts. Where it is not criticism
it moves towards cultural history and the sociology of literature, though I should like to think that all three approaches
can be kept in a coherent and mutually supportive relation.
The first chapter discusses the writers I am interested in
as a generational group, who shared important formative
experiences: being sons of the English or Anglo-Irish professional or administrative class, very conscious of the First
World War but too young to fight in it; educated at
boarding schools and, in nearly all cases, at Oxford or
Cambridge. This common experience seems to me more
important if less noticeable than the left-wing political views
attributed to the 'Auden Group'; it also characterised writers

who were apolitical or right-wing, like Graham Greene, Anthony Powell and Evelyn Waugh. This chapter draws on biographical material, but not quite in the way of conventional literary biography; I am more concerned with seeing how the text we call a writer's 'life' interacts with the other text we call his 'work', and with typical rather than individual elements. In subsequent chapters the emphasis is on common elements of style and structure, verbal and cultural. If texts are placed in their contexts, it is also suggested that the contexts, or other texts, can become important constituents of the texts themselves.

This book had, in fact, two points of departure. One of them was the interest in the typology and mythology of the thirties just referred to. The other, of a more theoretical kind, was interest in the nature of a literary period, and how far it can be described or even defined in terms of regular and recurring structural constituents. There are some relevant and suggestive remarks in Graham Hough's book *Style and Stylistics*:

> I am often haunted by the suspicion that the art historians, with their schools and styles and periods, have a command of their material and of its developments that literary historians seem to lack. And to many Continental students our unwillingness to deal in such ideas would seem but another example of our well-known incapacity for going beyond the barest empiricism.[1]

Since Hough wrote, English literary culture has become increasingly open to Continental ideas, so that a bare empiricism seems less wholly adequate than it once did, and words like 'generalisation', 'abstraction' and 'theory' seem less self-evidently condemnatory. I have tried to follow up the implications of Hough's words; in doing so I have been helped by some ideas, however imperfectly apprehended, of the late Lucien Goldmann. He emphasised 'group consciousness' and the way in which writers will express this consciousness, however much they think they are writing for themselves alone. Beyond a certain point I cannot follow Goldmann: in his Marxism (or, as some would have it, his left-Hegelianism); his insistence that significant social groups are social classes; and his belief that what makes writers great is their expression of the 'world vision' of an emergent social class. But, in appropriating ideas from their ideological context, I have found Goldmann a useful corrective to the familiar individualism and empiricism of English literary discourse. Goldmann directs attention to the 'trans-individual' mental structures involved in writing, and I have tried to do something similar in this book. I believe, though, that the individual talent is more important than Goldmann would allow; indeed, it is interesting to see how such very individual, even idiosyncratic modes of expression as those of W. H. Auden or Graham Greene still fit into and reproduce the mental and imaginative structures of the group. There is a further paradox, which I elaborate later, in the diffusion of Auden's style to such an extent that it became part of the cultural environment rather than the mark of a particular personality. Goldmann's ideas have some affinities with those of Raymond Williams, who has argued that a particular collective 'structure of feeling' can shape the literary expressions of a period; Williams too I have found useful. (He has set on record his own interest in Goldmann's theories about the 'collective subject', and the structures of the genesis of consciousness.[2])

Accounts of the literature of the 1930s often stress the closeness of that literature to social questions, under such headings as 'Literature and Society', or 'Literature and the social and/or political background'. I believe that it is right to examine the closeness of literary and social interests at that time, and I have done so in this book, but I have also tried to find a new way of relating them. In particular, I think we need to phase out the inert concept of 'background', however useful or even indispensable it is to planners of academic courses or writers of textbooks. The problem is that if the background appears important or interesting in the discussion of a text, then inevitably it comes to be part of the foreground. The most desirable change is in our model of the literary text. We are all familiar with the idea of the text as a smooth, solid, self-enclosed, free-standing object, the Well-Wrought Urn or Ver-

bal Icon of New Critical theory, placed some way in front
of its social, intellectual and historical 'background' so that
there seems to be no evident way of relating them. I
propose instead a more kinetic model, which makes the
text less tangible though no less specific; that is to say,
the text as a field of force, or configuration of energy,
or a vortex, to return to one of the dominant images
of high modernist poetics, as described by Hugh Kenner
in *The Pound Era*. I am influenced in this suggestion by
Roland Barthes's model of the text, in *S/Z*, as a system
of interlocking codes, of almost indefinite possible extension,
though I do not want to take over Barthes's scholastic
terminology, nor his attempted fusion of classical rhetoric
and psychoanalysis. But Barthes does help one to a more
open model of the text. If the text is a field of force
then its whirling constituents come from many possible
sources as well as the author's creative brain and imagination.

The Anglo-American critical tradition assumes that a
literary text is solely dependent upon its author; it exists,
simply, because a particular person has written it. Recent
Continental critics, by contrast, give the individual author
a very modest place among all the other determinants
of the text: the state of the language, the genre, the contemporary literary situation, the ideology of the author's social
group or class, the nature of productive relations in society
at large, the desires and expectations of the audience. In
our tradition, most of these elements would be relegated
to the background, to be looked into or ignored, according
to the reader's inclinations. But, in the model I propose,
all these elements—personal, intellectual, literary, linguistic,
social—would be there *in* the text, as constituent elements,
or part of the network of codes that make up the totality.
The uniquely personal element that we look for in a literary
work would consist in the form, the configuration or particular vortex, that informs all these constituents. In the case
of major talents it will be original and arresting; with
minor ones it will be conventional or imitative; and very
minor work can seem to have no author at all, to be
merely an emanation of the spirit of the age, so formulaic

is it. There are some instances of such writing in this book, and despite their aesthetic nullity they are useful in exemplifying in a simple state the collective style of the times, the *langue* from which the *parole* of unique artistic utterance is formed.

Here are some specific examples of how contexts enter texts, which I discuss more fully later. In the literature of the thirties there are frequent references to a possible war and the threat of bombing; and to the rituals of cinema-going and the cult of film-stars. They form prominent subtexts in novels or poems. One can never be certain, simply by inspecting a literary text, that things referred to in it are direct reflections of contemporary society or events; they may well have their origin in literary convention or a prevalent ideology. Yet, if references are scattered over a variety of texts, one gets the sense of a system building up, referring to, say, bombers, or film-stars. At that point one may move from literature to historical evidence and find that there was indeed a widespread fear of bombing or a cult of film-stars in the 1930s. The movement will involve an interaction between the texts of literature and the texts of history on particular topics, a more dynamic process than merely 'filling in the background'. And, since fields of force may interpenetrate, it is not surprising that literary texts may move in and out of each other, literature always drawing, in part, on other literature as well as on the larger world outside it.

Literary texts remain unique entities, but they inevitably enter into relations with other texts, either by the same author, in a context of personal development; or by other, contemporary authors, in a group context of shared attitudes and influences. So, too, in astronomy do single stars form constellations, and constellations form galaxies, even though, in the end, everything consists of single stars. In the present book I have tried to trace connections and interrelations to the extent that one can, ultimately and by a process of deliberate abstraction (which means no more than 'drawing out of'), speak of 'the thirties' as a collective text, the trans-individual product of a generation, possessing, like the *oeuvre* of an individual author, a number of regular and recurring features. I am still, however, sufficient of an Anglo-Saxon empiricist to remain sceptical of single, ultimately reductive explanations of diverse phenomena, whether in terms of a transcendent *Zeitgeist*, or the 'economic base' to which, 'in the last analysis', all cultural manifestations must be referred, however many 'mediations' have to be slotted in between text and base. I have looked for larger coherences than ordinary empirical readings can provide, but not final explanations.

I think it likely that survivors of the thirties generation, if they chance to read this book, will complain that everything they knew is distorted, that it was not like that at all. I remain unabashed: single stars may well believe that the universe consists of single stars and that talk of constellations and galaxies is so much nonsense. C. Day Lewis, for instance, remarked in his autobiography, *The Buried Day*, that, though throughout the thirties he and Auden and Spender were always regarded as a tight little group of poets, they did not all three meet in one room until 1947. One takes the point, whilst insisting that a group need not necessarily imply a circle of writers sitting round a café table composing a joint manifesto. A group can still be recognisable as such, even if the separate members rarely meet or do not know each other personally at all. My concern is not only with what was happening forty and more years ago, in all its diversity and detail; that has been fully and richly set down in biographies and memoirs. I have attempted, rather, to find categories and models to make sense of all that activity. For that matter, survivors, because of their particular allegiances, may make distorted judgements. There is a good example in the '1930s Special Number' of *Renaissance and Modern Studies* (1976). Arnold Rattenbury was too young to be very active in the thirties, but in the early forties he was friendly with several older Communist writers who had been. He writes in an essay called 'Total Attainder and the Helots',

Perhaps I put things poorly, being unaccustomed to memoir and polemic both; but orthodoxy lies and someone, if only a boy at the time, must say so. That

the Thirties were made of Auden and friends and such
influences as reached them is as unlikely a notion as
daft.[3]

To that unlikelihood and daftness I unrepentantly admit.
Although I make limiting judgements on Auden in the
following pages, his centrality in the literary life of the
thirties seems to me unmistakable. Unlike other hostile
critics of 'orthodoxy', Mr Rattenbury does give a hostage
to fortune by proposing an alternative. This proves to
be Randall Swingler, a minor Communist poet, a Wyke-
hamist and sometime editor of *Left Review* (whom I can
remember as a man of immense charm when I used to
attend his extra-mural lectures at Goldsmiths' College in
the early fifties): 'It's hard for me to say other than that
he wrote from a centre of his times, while Auden wrote
roundabout.' One can check Mr Rattenbury's judgement
at once, because that same issue of *Renaissance and Modern
Studies* contains a substantial selection of Swingler's poems.
Whatever their merits, Auden's centrality is unaffected.

I have not presented a single developing argument in
this book. It is, in form, a set of essays which consider
different aspects, or different cross-sections, of the literature
of the thirties, and which do not attempt to be exhaustive.
But certain themes emerge which I try to draw together
in the Conclusion. And, to repeat a remark made in the
opening sentence of this introduction, there are important
texts written between 1930 and 1940 that I say nothing
about. I reiterate this for the benefit of reviewers, who
when faced with a selective study of a subject are liable
to complain that it is not a comprehensive study, and
then list all the missing names. To save them trouble
I shall set down some names here and now. There is,
for instance, nothing about the later writings of the major
modernists, published during the decade: Eliot's 'Burnt Nor-
ton', Yeats's *Last Poems*, Joyce's *Finnegans Wake*, Virginia
Woolf's *The Waves*, Wyndham Lewis's *The Revenge for Love*.
Nor about remarkable new work by younger writers in
the modernist tradition, such as David Jones's *In Parenthesis*
or Samuel Beckett's *Murphy*. And there are only fleeting

references to slightly younger writers who began in the thirties and did not attend public schools, such as Dylan Thomas, George Barker and David Gascoyne. And nothing about the fine work of a Scottish Marxist who had some political affinities with the writers I do discuss, but little else in common: Lewis Grassic Gibbon's *A Scots Quair*. Some of these novels and poems I love and admire, at least as much as the texts I have chosen to discuss. But they belong on different maps, are to be sought on different expeditions.

1 Men Among Boys, Boys Among Men

The question, 'Where were you (or, Where was he) at school?' is not always, in an English context, a simple request for information. It often implies that the person addressed was at a public school, or might have been, and the answer will enable him to be fitted into the pattern of fine gradations that extends over upper-middle class and upper-class society. As has been often remarked, the crucial social division in England is not between middle and working class, but between the upper and lower middle class; between those who were educated at a grammar school, or no school in particular, and a public school, however minor. And the public school, in this scheme, is usually preceded by a preparatory school and followed by Oxford or Cambridge. This has been the traditional pattern for the professional and administrative classes in England, and for much of the aristocracy. It has never been general for men of letters, however: their social basis tends to be wider, stretching well down into the lower middle class and even, exceptionally, to the working class. We can consider the writers who were active in England in 1915, or at least bringing their work out from London publishers. It is a convenient year, since Henry James was still alive and writing then, and T. S. Eliot and Virginia Woolf published their first work. Some basic names include those of Joseph Conrad, Bernard Shaw, H. G. Wells, Rudyard Kipling, W. B. Yeats, Arnold Bennett, John Galsworthy, E. M. Forster, Ford Madox Ford, D. H. Lawrence, Wyndham Lewis, James Joyce and Ezra

Pound. Most of these writers, because of their social origin, nationality or sex, did not fit into the established educational pattern. A few went to public schools: Ford to University College School, Kipling to United Services College; and Wyndham Lewis, who was partly American, was at Rugby for two years. Only two went to ancient English universities: John Galsworthy, who was at Harrow and New College, Oxford; and Forster, at Tonbridge and King's, Cambridge. One might also mention the poet Rupert Brooke, who was at Rugby and King's, and was probably destined for an academic career when he died on active service in 1915.

If we move twenty years on, to the generation of young writers who were emerging in 1935, we see that what was previously an exception has now become the rule. These men were born in the first decade of the twentieth century, were at school during the First World War, and began to write and publish in the late twenties: Auden, Spender, Day Lewis, Betjeman, Lehmann and MacNeice, among poets; Isherwood, Upward, Waugh, Greene, Orwell, Powell, Connolly and Green, among novelists. Their educational formation was strikingly homogeneous: all of them went to public schools and, with one exception, to Oxford or Cambridge. The exception was the inveterate nonconformist George Orwell, who after leaving Eton joined the Indian Imperial Police. The sociological reasons for this marked increase in cultural homogeneity are a matter for speculation, but its literary implications are easy to see. These writers did in every sense have important things in common, in addition to generational identity and the four years of the Great War, which they experienced as boys but were too young to participate in. The culture of the English public school was intended to put a firm— ideally, ineradicable—stamp upon young men. The writers of the thirties did not escape the process; they were clearly marked, even though they spent much energy and effort in trying to escape that training and influence. For several of them the process was complicated by returning to the school world after leaving university, to earn a living by teaching in prep schools or public schools. So we find in the writing of the thirties the insistent presence of schools and schoolboys and schoolmasters as sources of imagery and theme and tone.

On the plane of biography, one can consider an example of the importance, in English upper middle-class life, of whom you get to know at school, a topic given brilliant, extended fictional treatment by Anthony Powell in *A Dance to the Music of Time*. As small boys Wystan Hugh Auden and Christopher Isherwood were at the same prep school, St Edmund's, Hindhead, Surrey. In *Lions and Shadows* (1938) Isherwood provides a lively, caricatural account of Auden as a boy, three years younger but already domineering and seemingly omniscient:

> To several of us, including myself, he confided the first naughty stupendous breath-taking hints about the facts of sex. I remember him chiefly for his naughtiness, his insolence, his smirking tantalizing air of knowing disreputable and exciting secrets. With his hinted forbidden knowledge and stock of mispronounced scientific words, portentously uttered, he enjoyed among us, his semi-savage credulous schoolfellows, the status of a kind of witch-doctor. I see him drawing an indecent picture on the upper fourth form blackboard, his stumpy fingers, with their blunt bitten nails, covered in ink; I see him boxing, with his ferocious frown, against a boy twice his size; I see him frowning as he sings opposite me in the choir, surpliced, in an enormous Eton collar, above which the great red flaps of ears stand out, on either side of his narrow scowling pudding-white face.[1]

After St Edmund's, the boys' paths diverged for a time, as they went on to different public schools, Auden to Gresham's, Isherwood to Repton. At Repton Isherwood made another vital and enduring friendship, with Edward Upward, the 'Chalmers' of *Lions and Shadows*. For Isherwood Upward was another influential, even manipulative figure. He appears in *Lions and Shadows* as 'a natural anarchist, a born romantic revolutionary', who hated the school and all established authority. Nevertheless, he won a history

scholarship to Corpus Christi College, Cambridge, to which
Isherwood went a year later. At Cambridge Isherwood
and Upward shared fantasies of conspiratorial revolt against
the university, continuing Upward's revolt against school.
These fantasies, of imaginary places called the 'Other Town'
and 'Rats' Hostel', and eventually 'Mortmere', can reason-
ably be called schoolboyish. The shared programme, as
Isherwood describes it, of mocking and attacking the university is in strong contrast to the tendency—which we find
in the early years of the century, in the Cambridge of
Forster and Rupert Brooke and Lytton Strachey—to idealise
Cambridge as a fine pinnacle of civilisation. But the war
had intervened, and brought a great transvaluation of values.
Isherwood had felt that he and all his generation, by
being too young for the war that had proved so crucial,
and sometimes fatal, an encounter for their fathers and
elder brothers had somehow missed a test, or The Test,
as Isherwood called it: 'Like most of my generation, I
was obsessed by a complex of terrors and longings connected
with the idea "War". "War", in this purely neurotic sense,
meant The Test. The test of your courage, of your maturity,
of your sexual prowess: "Are you really a Man?" ' So,
the War, or The Test, was transposed in Isherwood's fantasies into the familiar world of school:

> Gradually, in the most utter secrecy, I began to evolve
> a cult of the public-school system. It was no good, of
> course, pretending that my own school career had been
> in any sense romantic, heroic, dangerous, epic—that
> wasn't necessary. I built up the daydream of an heroic
> school career, in which the central figure, the dream
> I, was an austere young prefect, called upon unexpectedly
> to captain a 'bad' house, surrounded by sneering critics
> and open enemies, fighting slackness, moral rottenness,
> grimly repressing his own romantic feelings towards a
> younger boy, and finally triumphing over all his obstacles,
> passing the test, emerging—a Man. Need I confess any
> more? How, in dark corners of bookshops, I furtively
> turned the pages of adventure stories designed for boys
> of twelve years old? No illustration was too crudely

coloured, no yarn too steep for my consuming guilty
appetite.[2]

Isherwood's obsession may have been extreme, but something
rather like it became a commonplace in the writing of
the thirties, where the conventions and codes of the prep
school and public school are often used to convey serious
social and political attitudes. What Isherwood did not feel
able to be explicit about in *Lions and Shadows* was another
characteristic of the culture of the boarding school: homosexuality. Recently, though, he has done it ample justice in
Christopher and His Kind (1977).

In 1925, after he had left Cambridge, Isherwood resumed
his early friendship with Auden. At that time Auden was
an undergraduate at Christ Church, Oxford, was writing
poetry, and becoming known as the eccentric, authoritarian
figure described in the autobiographies of Stephen Spender
and Cecil Day Lewis. Through Isherwood Auden met
Upward, who appears to have influenced him in ways
so far unremarked. Thus, in *Lions and Shadows* Isherwood
quotes from a letter by Upward, written sometime in the
late twenties, which is Audenesque in language, imagery
and tone:

> the same boiling fraud hangs like an exhalation on tile
> and tree. O boy, I have the vision at last. I see the
> enormous calm disaster and the pouring tears. I stand
> by the matchwood scoring board in the sun and watch
> the awed fielders as they carry away the dead boy from
> the wicket. Ninety-nine runs. His white flannel trousers
> have grass stains at the knee. . . . Far away a paddle-
> steamer is stuck in the afternoon sea.[3]

And, as I show subsequently, there are similar phrases
in Auden's and Upward's contributions to *New Country*.
Auden and Isherwood found they had a common tendency
to look at the world in terms of school life; and, when,
on Auden's recommendation, Isherwood began to read the
Icelandic sagas, these seemingly remote narratives came
to seem strangely familiar:

These warriors, with their feuds, their practical jokes, their dark threats conveyed in puns and riddles and deliberate understatements ('I think this day will end unluckily for some, but chiefly for those who least expect harm') : they seemed so familiar—where had I met before? Yes, I recognized them now: they were the boys at our preparatory school.[4]

In time, Isherwood continues, he and Auden invented a fantasy world (which resembled Mortmere, devised by Isherwood and Upward at Cambridge) compounded of the sagas and memories of their prep school.

About a year later, I actually tried the experiment of writing a school story in what was a kind of hybrid language composed of saga phraseology and schoolboy slang. And soon after this, Weston [Auden] produced a short verse play in which the two worlds are so confused that it is almost impossible to say whether the characters are epic heroes or members of a school O. T. C. [Officers' Training Corps].[5]

Isherwood's story was 'Gems of Belgian Architecture', eventually published in *Exhumations* in 1966. It is a slight-enough piece, no more than a literary curiosity, though the style does what Isherwood claims for it, in combining the sagas and the school:

On the Saturday before Pay Day, the last Sunday in the Term, Dog and Griffin and Sale made up their minds that tomorrow they'd pay Dwight enough to satisfy him and slightly extra. Griffin was really the leader in this, but Sale and Dodgson were quite ready to back him up, whatever happened.

Sunday morning was cold and drizzling. Very few people went out into the grounds. Most of the Seniors stayed in the Library. Dwight was there, reading. After a few minutes, Dog Minor came in and told Dwight he was wanted down at the miniature range. Dwight seemed a bit suspicious. He asked: 'Who wants me?'

Dog Minor said: 'Mr. Roach.' Dwight had seen Fernandos
and Ringrose-Voase going down there that morning to
practise. Mr. Roach often took shooting and sent for
people he thought were slacking. Dwight hadn't been
to the range lately. So he decided it must be all right.
He started off at once.

Dog Major and Sale and Griffin were ambushed at
a narrow part of the path, well away from the house.
They came out and surrounded Dwight as he passed.
Griffin was carrying a piece of rope. Dwight said: 'Well,
what do you want?' Griffin said: 'It's Pay Day.' Dwight
said: 'Oh, that's a pity, isn't it?' Griffin said: 'Yes,
a great pity.'[6]

Auden's play, 'Paid on Both Sides', was a more serious
and innovatory piece of work, which attracted Eliot's attention and was published in *The Criterion*, launching Auden's
public career as a poet. It dramatises a feud between
two families, the Nowers and the Shaws, and is set in
the rugged country, partly Scandinavian, partly northern
English, that so appealed to Auden's imagination. The
play is very successful in fusing the bitter intensities of
the saga and the self-conscious heroics of school stories.
It is obscure but powerful, containing some of Auden's
best early poetry, including pieces taken over from his
privately printed *Poems* of 1928. 'Paid on Both Sides' was
included in the Faber *Poems* of 1930, which was dedicated
to Isherwood; in that collection there are other echoes
of the schoolboy world:

> The silly fool, the silly fool
> Was sillier in school
> But beat the bully as a rule　　(**XIX**)

or

> Far other than that distant afternoon
> Amid rustle of frocks and stamping feet
> They gave the prizes to the ruined boys.　　(**XXIX**)

Such references were later reinforced by Auden's own experience as a schoolmaster. Recently Isherwood has revealed a more personal schoolboyish element in his friendship with Auden. Discussing their relationship as it existed in 1937, he writes of them both in the third person:

> Their friendship was rooted in schoolboy memories and the mood of its sexuality was adolescent. They had been going to bed together, unromantically but with much pleasure, for the past ten years, whenever an opportunity offered itself, as it did now. They couldn't think of themselves as lovers, yet sex had given friendship an extra dimension. They were conscious of this and it embarrassed them slightly—that is to say, the sophisticated adult friends were embarrassed by the schoolboy sex partners.[7]

In 1928, at about the same time that Isherwood wrote 'Gems of Belgian Architecture' and Auden wrote 'Paid on Both Sides', Edward Upward completed the last and longest of the Mortmere stories, and the only one that has ever been published: 'The Railway Accident'. In *Lions and Shadows*, Isherwood gives quite a full account of Mortmere, as he and Upward devised it at Cambridge, with a list of its denizens. The first Mortmere character was the Reverend Welken, described as 'tall, very thin, with lank hair parted in the middle, he was once described as resembling a diseased goat'. His closest friend was Ronald Gunball, 'a frank unashamed vulgarian, a keen fisherman and a grotesque liar'. Others included Reynard Moxon and Dr Mears, Sergeant Claptree, Harry Belmare and his sister, and, a significant figure in 'The Railway Accident', Gustave Shreeve, headmaster of Frisbald College for boys. The Mortmere world brought together a rich variety of literary antecedents: boys' stories; Sherlock Holmes and other versions of the classical English detective story; Lewis Carroll; the Gothic novel. We do not know how the collaboration between Isherwood and Upward worked in practice, nor how extensive the literary remains of Mortmere are, apart from 'The Railway Accident'. (Some manuscripts

were displayed at the 'Young Writers of the Thirties' exhibition at the National Portrait Gallery in 1976, and I hope
that more material will one day be published.) In *Lions
and Shadows* Isherwood quotes the paragraph in which
Upward started writing about Mortmere:

> It has been said that Mortmere rectory does not seem
> to be the work of an architect, but to have grown
> as an oak grows, from the soil of the fields. There is
> scarcely a colour throughout the surrounding land that
> has not its counterpart in the garden and the rectory
> walls. In sunlight the blue-grey slates of the roof seem
> almost to reflect the leaves of the garden trees, much
> as the muddy village pond dimly reflects the elm-leaves
> that lift and dip above it. The red creepers obscuring
> the trellised supports of the veranda, even the grey cowls
> and the chimneys, have an appearance of continuity
> with the surrounding country. Not only the rectory, but
> the smaller houses and cottages of the village have this
> strange likeness to living growths of the soil. The Rector
> of Mortmere once said that, if every building were to
> be transplanted during the night, he would scarcely notice
> the change when he woke in the morning. . . .[8]

This seems to me remarkably assured, even distinguished,
prose. In 'The Railway Accident' what may have begun
as a private fantasy is transformed into literature, albeit
of a very strange and idiosyncratic kind. In a note on
'The Railway Accident' Isherwood has pertinently remarked

> Perhaps 'The Railway Accident' can best be described
> as a dream, or a nightmare, about the English; Gunball,
> Welken and Shreeve are all dream-distortions of classic
> English types. At moments they seem nearly normal,
> nearly convincing; and they appear to be taking each
> other quite seriously. But this is only a part of their
> basic social pretence. Life in Mortmere is like a poker-
> game between telepathists, in which everybody is bluffing
> and nobody is fooled.[9]

Though written in ignorance of the surrealists' dislocations of reality, or the logical nightmares of Kafka, 'The Railway Accident' offers a very English equivalent of both, and is, I think, one of the minor triumphs of twentieth-century English fiction. Most of the story is taken up with a bizarre railway journey to Mortmere, ending with a terrible accident from which, however, Hearn, the narrator, and his travelling companion, Gustave Shreeve, the headmaster, manage to escape. Shreeve, who is meticulous and overbearing and probably insane (though such a term has little meaning in the Mortmere world) is an exaggeratedly ideal type of the English schoolmaster. His opening remark, when Hearn notices him in the railway carriage, is characteristically self-defining: 'Well, I'll admit I slipped in rather on the quiet. Part of my trade you know. Otherwise you could never be sure what they weren't doing in the dormitories.' Later he remarks in conversation, 'Ten minutes late for an appointment and you lose a rattling good post in the colonies which would have made you for life.' And, when some soldiers in the next coach are making too much noise, Shreeve yells through the dividing door, 'Here, cheese that row you fellows.' Shreeve is wonderfully vivid, but he is, in the last analysis, a figure of fun, or fantasy. In Upward's later fiction, and in other writing of the thirties, the headmaster becomes a realistic embodiment of social and even political power.

'The Railway Accident' remained unpublished for many years. But it was widely circulated in manuscript among Isherwood's friends, and was particularly admired by Auden. John Lehmann has recalled in his autobiography that Auden used to quote from it in lectures.[10] Auden made evident use of Mortmere in his own writings. In *The Orators* (1932) he refers by name to two Mortmere characters, Moxon and Miss Belmare, and in both that work and *The Dog Beneath the Skin* (1935) the presentation of English life in terms of a deranged typicality recalls Mortmere. 'The Railway Accident' also emphasises the likelihood of specific stylistic influence by Upward upon Auden. Hearn's observations from the train produce the lists of typical social or natural detail, sharply and separately observed, that we find in Auden's poetry from 1930 onwards:

An airman in furs swung the propellor of a small mono-
plane. Someone was killing a rabbit with wire in the
spinney. Seagulls on arable land far from the sea estuary
circled for worms. A dung heap smoked in the damascene
steel air. Woods passed like frozen paper.[11]

Gustave Shreeve, like Auden, is a map-maker:

Shreeve was marking a corner of his map very heavily
with the pencil. And of all those boys who through
the changing years would constantly look up to him,
not one dreamed that in the privacy of his room their
headmaster was, profoundly and irretrievably, a coward.
Ploughed fields were succeeded by grass, a lake, a private
golf course. Gentleman's country. Here Disraeli wrote
his novels. Turf mounds rotted in the damp shadow
of the cypress avenue. The head gardener had invented
but could not afford to advertise a herbal balm for
eczema. It had cured the master and several of his
friends. There were iron railings round the trees.[12]

Such writing is very reminiscent of the prose sections of
The Orators. Upward spent all his working life as a schoolmaster; and he became a Marxist before any of his literary
friends, abandoning Mortmere as an escapist fantasy. Isherwood describes the movement from Mortmere to Marx
in these words:

He was to spend the next three years in desperate and
bitter struggles to relate Mortmere to the real world
of the jobs and the lodging-houses; to find the formula
which would transform our private fancies and amusing
freaks and bogies into valid symbols of the ills of society
and the toils and aspirations of our daily lives. For
the formula did, after all, exist. And Chalmers [Upward]
did at last find it, at the end of a long and weary
search, not hidden in the mysterious emblems of Dürer
or the prophetic utterances of Blake, not in any anagram,

or cipher, or medieval Latin inscription, but quite clearly set down, for everybody to read, in the pages of Lenin and of Marx.[13]

Upward published little in the thirties, but he remained an admired and mysterious figure to his contemporaries, something of an *éminence grise*, who was rightly believed to have been an important influence on Auden and Isherwood. Upward contributed two stories to *New Country*, 'Sunday' and 'The Colleagues'. Both read like imaginative accounts of a conversion to Marxism. 'The Colleagues' is set in a prep school, with overtones of Mortmere in style and atmosphere. The young schoolmaster who is the narrator loathes the school and his colleagues, and by the end of the story has undergone what would now be called a change of consciousness, which might eventually lead to revolutionary commitment. In *Journey to the Border*, published as a short novel in 1938, which I discuss in a later chapter, the central figure is a private tutor in a rich family rather than a schoolmaster, but there is a similar progress, via mental disturbance, from alienation and near despair to ideological commitment. After 1942 Upward published nothing for twenty years. Then, in 1962, when he would have been a new and unfamiliar name to many younger readers, he brought out a novel, *In the Thirties*.[14] As the title suggests, this is a work of typification and mythologising. Though lacking the brilliance of 'The Railway Accident', the novel is lucidly and sensitively written. It is clearly intended to be an imaginative re-enactment and recapitulation not just of Upward's own experience, but in some sense of his whole generation's. Again, the underlying story is simple: the young, middle-class poet Alan Sebrill finds he can no longer write, or live meaningfully, in the sterile world of bourgeois individualism. He becomes a Marxist, joints the Communist Party and finds that his life now has point and purpose. Meantime he is working as a schoolmaster in a boys' college with public-school pretensions, and manages with some difficulty to reconcile his beliefs with his work as a teacher. The opening parts of the novel, set in what is evidently the Isle of

Wight, where Alan is on holiday and trying to finish a long poem, recall earlier and related literary treatments of that part of England: by Isherwood in *Lions and Shadows* and his story 'An Evening at the Bay'; by Upward himself in 'The Island'; and by Auden in 'On This Island' and 'August for the People'. Upward's hero, Alan, has the calculated simplicity and naivety that we find in the central figures of Isherwood's first novels, *All the Conspirators* and *The Memorial*, and which Isherwood himself has freely acknowledged as derived from the early E. M. Forster. Yet a certain kind of naivety was part of the pervading cultural style of the thirties, as Martin Green has recently observed in *Children of the Sun*. He distinguishes the naive from the 'naif', remarking that '*Naif* does not mean the opposite of subtle, of course, but open to every experience, constantly and essentially responsive and potential.' This state of mind was not easily reconcilable with full adherence to the Communist Party of Great Britain, which is perhaps why so few literary men stayed in it for long. (Upward, however, remained a member for many years and only left in the late forties because he believed the Party was lacking in revolutionary fervour.) *In the Thirties* is a transparent but puzzling book, and in places the tone, whether the author's or Alan's, is almost unreadable. For instance, Alan reflects, soon after his conversion, 'The poet of today, if only he would turn to the Party, need no longer be ineffectual. Already over one sixth of the earth the Party had led the worker to victory against the enemies of poetry, and it would do the same in England.' One notes the period sentiments, which would have been commonplace in, say, the *Left Review* in the years when, in the Soviet Union, Osip Mandelshtam was undergoing persecution and eventual liquidation. But in a novel published in 1962 one might have expected some hint of distancing, if not of outright irony, in the presentation of such extravagantly naive propaganda. Yet I cannot detect such distancing in Upward's novel. The final episode is, however, historically ironical even though Upward gives no literary hints of irony. Alan Sebrill has found in the Communist Party not only ideological conviction but also warmth and human companionship.

Indeed he falls in love with and marries one of the Party workers, a young teacher at an elementary school. In the final pages of *In the Thirties*, Alan and his wife, Elsie, are on a country ramble with a group of Party members. He basks in his sense of their solid worth, as fighters for a cause and human beings. They are indeed the salt of the earth. Alan's feelings are like those expressed by Day Lewis in 'The Road These Times Must Take', a sonnet in Hopkinsese published in the *Left Review* in 1934:

Yes, why do we all, seeing a communist, feel small? That small
Catspaw ruffles our calm—how comes it? That touch of storm
Brewing, shivers the torches even in this vault? And the shame
Unsettles a high esteem? Here it is. There fall
From him shadows of what he is building; bold and tall—
For his sun has barely mastered the misted horizon—they seem.
Indeed he casts a shadow, as among the dead will some
Living one. It is the future walking to meet us all.

Mark him. He is only what we are, mortal. Yet from the night
Of history, where we lie dreaming still, he is wide awake:
Weak, liable to ill-luck—yet rock where we are slight
Eddies, and amid us islands the spring tide beginning to make.
Mark him workers, and all who wish the world aright—
He is what your sons will be, the road these times must take.[15]

(This provoked a savage response from a poet at the opposite end of the political spectrum, Roy Campbell:

Day Lewis to the Communist 'feels small'
But nothing's made me feel so steep and tall:
With me such things are easy to determine
Who never felt this reverence for vermin

> And all I know is, communists or germs,
> He fares the best who never comes to terms![16])

Yet Upward's idyllic episode is five years later, being set in July 1939. Within a few weeks would come the shattering announcement of the pact between Hitler and Stalin, closely followed by the outbreak of the Second World War. The Russo-German pact brought confusion and a sense of betrayal to many Communists, in England and elsewhere. One wonders how Alan Sebrill's happy, heroic rambling companions were destined to react to this perplexing event.

In the Thirties exemplifies a common theme in its treatment of Alan's experiences as a schoolmaster. He has to learn to keep discipline, and to put up with his fellow-teachers, many of whom are very reactionary. At one point he is summoned to an interview by the Headmaster, because of his failure with discipline. In the description of this interview Upward allows himself a single fleeting flash of Mortmere-like whimsy, indeed of private joking:

> At last, releasing into his tone a little of the exasperation he had probably been feeling all the time, the Head said, 'Really you ought not to be having this trouble with discipline. After all, you yourself as a boy were educated at Reptile'—he quickly corrected this—'I mean at Repton.'[17]

Upward himself, we recall, had been at Repton, and there began his revolt against established educational forms and institutions. There are remarkable anticipations of the typifying aspects of *In the Thirties* in Cecil Day Lewis's novel *Starting Point*, published in 1937. Like Upward, Day Lewis was for some time both a schoolmaster and a member of the Communist Party. His novel follows the changing fortunes of a group of Oxford friends during the ten years from 1926 to 1936. The central figure is Anthony Neale whom we first encounter as an undergraduate. He serves as a strikebreaker in the General Strike, when he has a troubling encounter with one of the workers' leaders, which eventually pushes him towards the political Left.

Anthony's father, Sir Charles Neale, is a Liberal politician and rentier who loses much of his money in the Depression and has to sell the beautiful family house in the Cotswolds. Anthony then becomes a schoolmaster and a Marxist, though for some time he remains a fellow-traveller rather than a Party member, still troubled by vestigial liberal doubts and ideas of open-mindedness. Like Upward's Alan Sebrill, Anthony is increasingly under attack by colleagues because of his political beliefs, and he too is summoned to an interview with the Head. And in both novels Lenin's *Material-ism and Empirio-Criticism* is a key text for the Communist neophyte. Eventually Anthony becomes a fully committed Communist and at the end of the book goes off to fight in Spain. The final paragraph is an emphatic propagandist flourish:

> These men and women—the oppressed, the anonymous, the workers—history had called them out of the ranks and given them her secret orders: they were the spies she sent forward into a hostile country, a land whose promise perhaps they alone could fully realize. They did not suppose that a paradise could be created by pressing a button or by fasting and prayer, nor did they expect flowers to spring up where they trod. He had seen them working with the furious diligence of beavers, the unobtrusive patience of the mole. Whether their hands were grained with coal-dust, marked with occupational scars, or pallid from the stagnant air of offices—it was these hands, Anthony believed, which would guide a new world struggling out of the womb. They would live and die and be forgotten: but their lives would be built into the deep foundations of the future. Of these he was one. With these he was one.

This passage is interesting not for any aesthetic reason, but as an example of the collective, virtually anonymous style of the time. Yet here as elsewhere the anonymity is broken by characteristically Audenesque locutions: 'the furious diligence of beavers, the unobtrusive patience of the mole'.

Auden himself succeeded Day Lewis as a master in a prep school at Helensburgh in Scotland, where he taught for several years. At Helensburgh he wrote a good but now somewhat inaccessible poem, 'A Happy New Year', which was printed in full only in *New Country* in 1933, though a much truncated version of the second section appears in *Collected Shorter Poems* as 'The Watchers'. 'Happy New Year' begins with Auden's particular situation as a schoolmaster, then projects a collective fantasy about the present state of England, which falls somewhere between the urgent but obscure jokiness of *The Orators* and the more relaxed, public style of 'Letter to Lord Byron'. The poem has an admirably assured and expansive opening, where the experience of the schoolmaster is swept up into Auden's characteristic topographical imagery:

> The third week in December frost came at last
> Into a windless morning I stepped and passed
> Outside the windows of untidy rooms
> Where boys were puzzled by exams,
> The ridges cloudless and the day my own.
> The Clyde untilted as I climbed;
> Boom of a distant siren skimmed
> Over the water like a well-shied stone.

The Orators itself, also written at Helensburgh, is Auden's most ambitious development of a state of mind and feeling that owes much to Mortmere and to boys' stories, in an attempt to anatomise England, 'This country of ours where nobody is well'. Schoolboy rhetoric and fantasies are pervasive, as in the list of miscellaneous disasters: 'Form-masters find crude graphite on their blackboards; the boys, out of control, imbibe Vimto through india-rubber tubing, openly pee into the ink-pots.' Of the six odes that form Book III of the original edition of *The Orators*, Ode II is dedicated 'To Gabriel Carritt, Captain of Sedbergh School XV, Spring, 1927', and vigorously describes a school rugger match; Ode III is dedicated to 'Edward Upward, Schoolmaster'; and Ode V 'To My Pupils'. In this ode Auden allows himself graver reflections than in most of *The Orators*:

Your childish moments of awareness were all of our world,
At five you sprang, already a tiger in the garden,
At night your mother taught you to pray for our Daddy
        Far away fighting,
One morning you fell off your horse and your brother
   mocked you:
        'Just like a girl!'

The most sustained evocation of the school world in *The
Orators* is in the first section, 'Address for a Prize-Day'.
The speaker is a distinguished Old Boy, returned to distribute
prizes. The Address is a virtuoso prose performance, which
brilliantly captures the register and tone of such a speech,
whilst analysing the condition of England, the sick organism,
in a way which makes full use of Auden's taste for geographical description. The speech begins with these words:

> Commemoration. Commemoration. What does it mean?
> What does it mean? Not what does it mean to them,
> there, then. What does it mean to us, here, now? It's
> a facer, isn't it boys? But we've all got to answer it.
> What were the dead like? What sort of people are we
> living with now? Why are we here? What are we going
> to do? Let's try putting it another way.

Auden, as a schoolmaster, would no doubt have listened
to his share of such speeches. But, if Isherwood is to be
believed, he was also recalling his own days at a prep
school. In *Lions and Shadows* Isherwood describes the undergraduate Auden comically imitating a preacher in the chapel
at St Edmund's: 'Sn Edmund's Day .... Sn Edmund's
Day .... Whur ders it *mean*? Nert—whur did it mean
to *them*, *then*, *theah*? Bert—whur ders it mean to *ers*, *heah*,
nerw?'
   Auden set down some balanced reflections on the public-
school system, and his own school, Gresham's, in particular,
in an essay he contributed to a collection edited by Graham
Greene, *The Old School*, in 1934. In the course of it he
remarked,

I have no wish to belittle a profession to which I have
the honour to belong. Its members are practically all
extremely conscientious, hard working, keen on their job,
and sometimes very intelligent. At the same time if one
were invited to dine with a company representing all
trades and professions, the schoolmaster is the last person
one would want to sit next to. Being a schoolmaster
is not like being a Bank Clerk—it is not enough just
to be efficient at teaching; one must be a remarkable
person. Some schoolmasters are, but far, far too many
are silted-up old maids, earnest young scoutmasters, or
just generally dim.

Some of the reasons for this are clear; in the first
place the profession has generally to be entered young,
and those of university age who are attracted to it are
rarely the most vital and adventurous spirits. On the
contrary they are only too often those who are afraid
of the mature world, either the athletic whose schooldays
were the peak of their triumph from which they dread
to recede, or else the timid academic whose qualifications
or personal charm are insufficient to secure them a fellow-
ship; in either case the would-be children.[18]

As Auden was well aware, the schoolmaster could have
an uncomfortably close relation with, even dependence upon,
those he taught: as the traditional jibe had it, he was
a boy among men, a man among boys. Yet this ambivalent
figure was to become something of a constituent literary
element of the period, and the source of some of its most
pervasive rhetoric.

The book in which Auden's essay appears is itself interesting evidence of a prevalent preoccupation with schools.
As well as Auden, the contributors to *The Old School* included
other young writers of the early thirties, such as Stephen
Spender, William Plomer and Anthony Powell, and the
editor, Graham Greene. Most of the contributors had
attended public schools, though there was a token account
of another section of the educational system, where Walter
Greenwood, author of *Love on the Dole*, recalled Langworthy
Road Council School, Salford. The emphasis, though, was

largely on the public school, and in his preface Graham
Greene expressed the remarkably erroneous conviction that
within a few years the public-school system would disappear.
Hence the justification of his collection: 'Where then but
in this book will the social historian discover a true picture
of the vanished system?' It is particularly interesting that
Greene should have been responsible for this book: the
English public school, particularly the minor or unsuccessful
one, is part of his personal mythology. Certainly his own
strange, divided schooldays at Berkhamstead have long been
an object of almost obsessive concern to him. He writes
about them in his contribution to *The Old School*, in *The
Lawless Roads* (1939), and in *A Sort of Life* (1971). Here,
as elsewhere in Greene, deeply personal preoccupations inter-
sect with the public ones of his age. Greene himself never
worked as a schoolmaster, though he came close to it.
Like Isherwood and others of his contemporaries he presented himself soon after graduating to the famous scholastic
agents Gabbitas and Thring. Greene remarked in *A Sort
of Life*, 'I had a horror of becoming involved in teaching',
partly because that was his father's profession. He did
work briefly as vacation tutor to a small boy, then escaped
into journalism. Yet the prep school and the public school
recur as sub-texts in his fiction. As, for instance, in *Stamboul
Train* (1932), where the political exile Dr Czinner, attempting to return to Yugoslavia to lead a revolution, recalls,
when he is arrested, his experiences as a schoolmaster in
England:

> He saw himself for a moment facing a desert of pitch-pine
> desks, row on row of malicious faces, and he remembered
> the times when he had felt round his heart the little
> cold draughts of disobedience, the secret signals and spurts
> of disguised laughter threatening his livelihood, for a
> master who could not keep order must eventually be
> dismissed. His enemies were offering him the one thing
> he had never known, security. There was no need to
> decide anything. He was at Peace. (Part IV, ch. 3)

In *England Made Me* (1935), arguably Greene's finest novel

of the thirties, the public school provides a prominent
constituent code. The central figure, or anti-hero, Anthony
Farrant, is a drifting sponger, unable to hold down a
job, who is sustained by memories of life at his minor
public school. His stream of consciousness is full of recollections of dormitories and prefects and housemasters. At the
beginning of the novel his sister Kate sees him as still
a schoolboy:

> His face, she thought, is astonishingly young for thirty-
> three; it is a little worn, but only as if by a wintry
> day, it is no more mature than when he was a schoolboy.
> He might be a schoolboy now, returned from a rather
> cold and wearing football match.   (Part I, ch. 1)

Anthony wears a Harrow tie to which he is not entitled,
and in Stockholm he meets a real Harrovian, the expatriate
journalist Minty, who in turn is trying to persuade the
British Minister, Sir Ronald, another Harrovian, to preside
at an Old Boys' dinner. Minty soon detects Anthony's
fraudulence, but nevertheless feels an increasing affinity
with him. At the end of the story, when Anthony is dead,
Minty produces a silver match-box engraved with the Harrow arms which he wished he had given Anthony: 'I
was really at Harrow, so it's no good to me. He'd have
liked it.' In a later novel, *Brighton Rock* (1938), there is
a curious marginal intrusion of a similar preoccupation,
when the crooked solicitor, Mr Prewitt, drunkenly tries
to interest Pinkie in a school photograph on his wall:

> 'Do you see that photo there—by the door? A school
> group. Lancaster College. Not one of the great schools
> perhaps, but you'll find it in the Public Schools Year
> Book. You'll see me there—cross-legged in the bottom
> row. In a straw hat.' He said softly. 'We had field
> days with Harrow. A rotten set they were. No *esprit
> de corps*.'   (Part VII, ch. 3)

Of the writers of that generation who had little sympathy
with the work and ideas of Auden and his disciples, there

were some who shared their interest in schools. George
Orwell was one. As a boy he attended a prep school
near Eastbourne called St Cyprian's. He was intensely miser-
able there and as an adult wrote a long autobiographical
essay about his schooldays, 'Such, Such were the Joys',
that recreated them with vivid, detailed loathing. After
St Cyprian's, Eton, to which Orwell went on a scholarship,
was a relatively happy experience. Cyril Connolly, who
was at St Cyprian's with Orwell, opposed in principle
the idea of sending small boys away to boarding school,
but still found St Cyprian's 'a well run and vigorous example
which did me a world of good'. But, as he recalled, 'I
was a stage rebel, Orwell a true one.' Connolly's *Enemies
of Promise*, in which these recollections appear, illustrates
my present argument. First published in 1938, it surveys
the contemporary literary scene and discusses the problem
of writing a book that will endure; it is in keeping with
the spirit of the age that Connolly should devote the last
third of his book to an autobiographical account of his
schooldays at St Cyprian's—there called St Wulfric's—and
Eton. Orwell, as a young man trying to establish himself
as a writer and needing employment, did what so many
others had done and took himself to a scholastic agent—Truman and Knightly, rivals to Gabbitas and Thring—in search
of a teaching post. His application resulted in a job in
a dismal prep school at Hayes on the Middlesex fringe
of London, where he taught for over a year. In the words
of his biographers, Peter Stansky and William Abrahams,
'After so many years to be back again in the ambience
of St. Cyprian's darkened his view of everything: the school
was "foul", the boys "brats", and Hayes "godforsaken".'
Orwell later made fictional use of the school, in the long,
bitter description in *A Clergyman's Daughter* of Dorothy Hare's
experience as a teacher in a similar establishment. Here,
as so often in Orwell's fiction, the essayist tends to take
over from the novelist, as in the paragraph beginning,

> There are, by the way, vast numbers of private schools
> in England. Second-rate, third-rate and fourth-rate (Ring-
> wood House was a specimen of the fourth-rate school)

they exist by the dozen and the score in every London suburb and every provincial town. (Ch. 4)

Such places were at some remove from the status and institutionalised glamour of the public schools. Nevertheless, they were part of the same system, since their aim was to prepare boys—and sometimes girls—for the Common Entrance Examination to the public schools.

One writer who taught briefly in a prep school and turned the experience into a literary classic was Evelyn Waugh. He, too, signed on at Truman and Knightly soon after leaving Oxford, and was sent to a school called Arnold Lodge in Denbighshire, north Wales, where he taught for the first half of 1925. He seems to have found the experience more endurable than Orwell did, perhaps because he took the work less seriously. According to accounts quoted by Christopher Sykes in his life of Waugh, he appeared at Arnold House as an amiable and mildly eccentric young man, whose working attire always included baggy plus-fours. Waugh's characteristically deadpan impressions of his teaching career are preserved in his diaries. But for most readers the school is memorably transformed into Llanabba Castle in *Decline and Fall*, the location of Paul Pennyfeather's inglorious career as a schoolmaster. The splendid Captain Grimes appears to have had a real-life original, called Young in the diaries.

The experience of school is both private and shared, a source of personal fantasies and public metaphors. In this ambivalent sense, the school is prominent, as institution or symbol, in the writing of the thirties. I want, finally, to consider ways in which the idea of the school related to the political concerns of the time. The literary converts to Communism felt the need to instruct, even to preach, and in such didactic exercises it was easy enough to slip into a schoolmasterly tone, particularly for those of them who actually were schoolmasters. In his essay in *The Old School* Auden suggested one way in which experience of school might relate to the political situation. He wrote, 'the best reason I have for opposing Fascism is that at school I lived in a Fascist state'. In the 'Address for a

Prize Day' in *The Orators* the school is a microcosm of
the sick society in need of revolutionary change:

> You've got some pretty stiff changes to make. We simply
> can't afford any passengers or skrimshankers. I should
> like to see you make a beginning before I go, now,
> here. Draw up a list of rotters and slackers, of proscribed
> persons under headings like this. Committees for municipal
> improvement—the headmaster. Disbelievers in the
> occult—the school chaplain. The bogusly cheerful—the
> games master—the really disgusted—the teacher of
> modern languages. All these have got to die without
> issue. Unless my memory fails me there's a stoke hole
> under the floor of this hall, the Black Hole we called
> it in my day. New boys were always put in it. Ah,
> I see I am right. Well look to it. Quick, guard that
> door. Stop that man. Good. Now boys hustle them,
> ready, steady—go.

The speaker, as a distinguished Old Boy, is easily able
to combine the verbal registers of schoolboy and schoolmaster, which are not, in any case, very far apart. The idea
may be revolution, but the language is of a schoolboy
rag. The situation and the tone proved easily imitable.
There is a good example in Ruthven Todd's fantastic novel
Over the Mountain (1939). The hero, Mr Michael, has been
invited to address a boys' school about his mountaineering
exploits. He begins in a manner appropriate to the occasion,
but he soon launches into a subversive tirade:

> 'Look around you at your well-fed companions, your
> natty Head and suave and soldierly Colonel Roscoe there.
> What do you think that they are doing to set these
> obvious wrongs right? Are they just content to let things
> slide? No, they are not letting things slide, and they
> are not doing their best to make things better for every
> one. They are actively fighting against the men who
> are trying to improve matters a little. They are the
> evil creatures that make oppression worse, the men who
> tread on the fallen. There are no rules for them in

the fight. They'll hit a man when he's down. They'll
deliver the blow beneath the belt, the elbow planted
in the kidneys in a clinch, the butt with the bullet
head, and the rabbit-punch behind the ears. They do
this because they are safe. The referee has turned his
back and is not interested in the fight. You—all of
you—are the referee. What is your decision, gentlemen?
Are they disqualified?"[19]

Both Day Lewis and Upward, writing in a didactic
vein, exemplify the tone of the Marxist schoolmaster. Here,
for instance, are extracts from Day Lewis's 'Letter to a
Young Revolutionary' (published in *New Country*), which
echoes (and quotes from) *The Orators*:

You have not joined the Communist Party as an act
of self-defence, defence against self, as though it were
nice to get it all off one's chest, to run to mother
and be told what to think and what to do, to have
the big bogy-man 'freedom' locked up in the cupboard
for good! You'll find some of this sort amongst your
comrades, men who have performed an act of funk,
not an act of faith. Tell them to come off it. They'll
only get in the way of you who are positive agents.[20]

Cut out that personal religion; those enervating dreams;
visions of tractors advancing over the sky-line and hedges
between fields and men going down; phantasies of yourself
in Russian blouse and peaked cap, persuading the English
to give up their possessions and plough for others to
reap. It won't pass. If you join the Communist Party
you'll have to wear a stiff collar and get down to some
hard labour.[21]

But when it comes to the point will you, Jonathan Smith,
be able to let off a revolver at Thomas Brown, bloated
capitalist, cad, liar, bully, beast and public nuisance
though you believe him to be? You can't go challenging
him to a duel, remember; it's you or him, and the
devil take the hindmost; back-street, hole-and-corner stuff;

a rat's death for a loser.[22]

Edward Upward, in his urgent, expository vein, is very similar; as in this extract from 'The Island', first published in *Left Review* in 1935:

> Perhaps you will do nothing here, perhaps you will never succeed in throwing off the exhaustion and worry of the past, you are too weak, too injured to recover, perhaps you are done for.
> What morbid bunk! This is the result of indulging in freakish fantasies and getting above yourself. Who but a fool would want to be a Greek? Come out of that sickly dreamland, that paradisal island of culture and everlasting joy, come and see the island as it really is, and make the best of the ordinary human pleasures it has to offer you. Stop thinking and start moving, jump into a train or motor-coach or on to your cycle, rush, drive, ride through the bright countryside, through woods, over bridges, down lanes, away to a real destination.[23]

One still detects, through such intensely serious injunctions, the shrill tones of Gustave Shreeve, headmaster of Frisbald College, Mortmere.

One remarkable young man did act out in reality Auden's notion that being at a public school gives one a particular motive for opposing fascism, making a rapid transition from schoolboy rebellion to fighting in a real war. This was Esmond Romilly, whose short and colourful life is described by Philip Toynbee in his affectionate but mythologising memoir *Friends Apart* (1954). Esmond Romilly came of a good family and was a nephew of Winston Churchill; whilst only fifteen he ran away from Wellington College to live a bohemian life in London. He started a magazine called *Out of Bounds*, whose manifesto proclaimed,

> *Out of Bounds* is against Reaction, Militarism and Fascism in the Public Schools. We attack not only the vast machinery of propaganda which forms the basis of the

public school system, and makes them so useful in a vicious and obsolete form of society; we oppose not only the semi-compulsory nature of the O. T. C. and the hypocritical bluff about 'character-building'. We oppose every one of the absurd restrictions and petty rules and regulations which would be more applicable to a kindergarten than to boys between the ages of fourteen and nineteen.[24]

Out of Bounds circulated widely in public schools for a time, and achieved fame or notoriety as a focus for rebellion. Two years later Romilly transferred the struggle to a dangerous and adult plane, when he went to Spain as a volunteer for the International Brigade. He took part in savage fighting on the outskirts of Madrid in December 1936, and wrote a book about it, *Boadilla*, which the historian of the Spanish Civil War, Hugh Thomas, has called 'an inspired description of the battle'. Romilly's later entertaining adventures are described in Philip Toynbee's book. He eloped with and married Jessica Mitford, the rebel daughter of Lord Redesdale. Then the couple were evacuated against their will from the embattled Basque Provinces by a British destroyer. Romilly, still a very young man, worked for a while as a salesman of silk stockings and an advertising copywriter. He and his wife went to America in 1939 and ran a bar in Miami. During the Second World War Romilly joined the Canadian Air Force and was killed in a bombing raid on Germany.

Few could move so directly from opposing the 'fascism' of the public school to taking arms against the real thing. Nevertheless, Auden's remark would have made sense to many of his contemporaries who had shared his early experience, and school metaphors seemed to occur naturally in discussions of politics. Thus, the acute Marxist critic Edgell Rickword remarked in an essay in the *Left Review* in 1934, 'And what are Hitler, Mosley or Mussolini like, more than those big backward boys who in every school get stuck in the Fourth Form, and who by a mixture of bullying and toadying attract a certain amount of unattached idealism to themselves?'[25] Europeans who knew something about fascism at first hand might have been puzzled by such imagery. But then the whole English boarding-school system, its mores and conventions, has always been puzzling—though often fascinating, too—to those who were not brought up within it. John Strachey, also writing in the *Left Review*, began his essay 'The Education of a Communist' with these words:

> I have a stock answer to dear old ladies who ask me, 'And why, Mr. Strachey, did you become a Communist?' 'From chagrin, madam,' I reply, 'from chagrin at not getting into the Eton Cricket Eleven.'
>
> I do not want this answer to be taken quite literally, except by the old ladies. All the same, there is in it more truth—if one takes getting into the Eton Cricket Eleven as a symbol for making an adjustment to one's environment as a whole—than I altogether enjoy admitting.[26]

Never before or since have English writers been so heavily marked by the homogeneous educational formation of the English upper and upper-middle classes. It provided a potent source of myth or allusion, and a figure of fun or sympathy in the ambivalent schoolmaster–schoolboy, in both aspects the prisoner of an institution. It also provided, at a time of strong political passions, a tone and rhetoric in which it was very difficult to express political convictions seriously.

2 Auden and the Audenesque

Auden's death in 1973 evoked some backward glances at his early career but no fresh appraisals. He had been described for many years as the leader of a group of poets who dominated English poetry in the 1930s, who were socially and politically conscious in a left-wing way, were influenced by Marx and Freud, and wrote about public themes: abandoned pits and factories; pylons and locomotives; unemployment at home and the rise of fascism in Europe; the Spanish Civil War. If the account has been added to, it has usually been in the direction of biography, drawing on the descriptions of Auden as a dominating young poet at Oxford provided in the autobiographies of Christopher Isherwood, Stephen Spender and Cecil Day Lewis. The emphasis has, in short, been thematic and generalised, or biographical and historical. Not much has been said about the way in which Auden's influence was as much stylistic as thematic. Auden's legacy from the thirties was not only his own dazzling and mannered poetry, but an instantly recognisable idiom, the 'Audenesque', which began with a few imitators early in the decade but within ten years was common throughout the English-speaking world. Karl Shapiro wrote in his long literary-critical poem *Essay on Rime* (1945) (Shapiro uses 'rime' in its old sense as an equivalent for 'poetry', and sometimes for 'poetics'),

The man whose impress on our rhetoric
Has for a decade dominated verse
In London, Sydney and New York is Auden.
One cannot estimate the consequences
Both good and bad of his success. To open
A current magazine of rime is but
To turn to Auden; and this is not a fad
But some kind of distemper in the practice
Of modern poetry.[1]

Not everything in Auden's own poetry was 'Audenesque'. From the beginning he had been a protean master of forms with not one style but many. To quote Shapiro again,

> Auden, a man of many aptitudes
> And that convincing artistry which draws
> A following, himself has set us models
> So variform as to deny identity
> To style.[2]

Auden's *Poems* of 1930 contained poems that resisted wide imitation, particularly the love poems, or the cryptic reflective pieces written in short lines, with a compact or repetitive syntax. It is only in his second collection, *Look, Stranger!* (1935), that one sees the full emergence of the Audenesque, by which I mean that particular manner of Auden's that became a collective idiom. Cecil Day Lewis was Auden's first unabashed disciple and imitator. They became acquainted at Oxford, where, although Auden was three years younger, Day Lewis succumbed heavily to his influence, particularly in 1927-8, when Auden was in his final undergraduate year and Day Lewis, having already graduated, was teaching in a prep school in north Oxford. Under Auden's dominance Day Lewis's verse changed rapidly from a neo-Georgian to an Audenesque manner; one of the sections of Day Lewis's *Transitional Poem* of 1929 contains an epigraph from Auden, while *The Magnetic Mountain* (1933) closely imitates Auden for long stretches at a time. By contrast, Stephen Spender, also much influ-

enced by Auden at Oxford, possessed a tougher and more
individual poetic personality; Auden's influence was more
thoroughly absorbed and was more apparent in themes
and choice of subject than in verbal mannerism, although
an occasional line like 'Northwards the sea exerts his huge
mandate', from 'The Port', in Spender's *Poems* (1933), is
a pure example of the Audenesque. Louis MacNeice, who
is often placed with Spender and Day Lewis as part of
the 'Auden group', seems to have known Auden only casually
at Oxford and to have developed independently as a poet.
His close contact with Auden did not begin until they
collaborated in *Letters from Iceland* in 1936.

It was the anthologies *New Signatures* (1932) and *New
Country* (1933) that found Auden a wider audience and
spread his influence. One of the contributors to the latter,
Charles Madge, wrote in his 'Letter to the Intelligentsia',

But there waited for me in the summer morning
Auden, fiercely. I read, shuddered and knew
And all the world's stationary things
In silence moved to take up new positions . . . .

The Supplement to the *Oxford English Dictionary* cites the
first occurrence of 'Audenesque' in a quotation from *Scrutiny*
in 1940. This is far too late: the word occurs much earlier,
in the title of Gavin Ewart's 'Audenesque for an Initiation'
published in *New Verse* in December 1933. (Admittedly
the word is generally an adjective, while Ewart here used
it as a noun, similar to 'humoresque'. Graham Greene
used it as an adjective in a film review in 1936.) This
poem, a remarkable achievement for a schoolboy of seven-
teen, as Ewart then was, is a witty and spirited imitation
of Auden's 'Get there if you can . . .' from the 1930 *Poems*
(itself, of course, a parody of Tennyson's 'Locksley Hall').
A few months later Ewart gave further evidence both of
his own fascination with Auden and of the way in which
Auden's name and influence were increasingly taken for
granted. In 'Journey' (*New Verse*, April 1934) Ewart wrote,

Where do I want to go? Let me see the map.
All these roads are Auden's, old chap.
I've been over them once, following his tracks;
The private paths are Eliot's, stony and complex . . . .

In using the image of the map, Ewart shrewdly directed
attention to a major feature of Auden's imaginative universe,
and one of the most influential. Landscapes and maps,
lists and catalogues, were indeed a recurring element in
Auden's poetry. But to make the point too baldly is to
emphasise content rather than form; critics of Auden have
written freely about industrial landscapes, abandoned work-
ings, or the airman's eye-view, but have not looked very
closely at the way his style worked and what its implications
were. One critic who did have an accurate understanding
of the Audenesque, considered primarily as style, was G.
Rostrevor Hamilton, whose short book *The Tell-Tale Article*,
published in 1949, contains some acute if generally unsym-
pathetic criticism of Auden. Hamilton drew attention to
the heavy concentration of definite articles in Auden and
other twentieth-century poets, and supported his analysis
with some comparative statistics. After working through
an anthology of English poetry in several volumes Hamilton
noted that, whereas from the eighteenth century to the
early twentieth the percentage of definite articles remained
constant at about 6 per cent, in the volume devoted to
modern poetry the percentage increased to 8½ per cent,
and rose to 10 per cent each for Eliot and Auden. By
contrast, in the poetry of the sixteenth and seventeenth
centuries the use of the definite article averages 4 per
cent, while in a large sample of Donne it is as low as
2 per cent. Hamilton argues that before the eighteenth
century poetry was less concerned with reflection and description and more with enacting relationships, whether
with God or man or woman, a mode that makes much
less of the definite article. On the other hand, in eighteenth
century descriptive poetry the percentage is of modern pro-
portions. 11 per cent for Thomson and 9 per cent for
Crabbe.[3]
The definite article points to the recognisable if not

to the already known. It recalls an actually or possibly
shared experience, as well as, in its twentieth-century uses,
reflecting the preference of modernist poetics for the particular against the general. This, as Hamilton points out, may
be based on a confusion, assuming that the opposition
'particular/general' is the same as the opposition 'sharp/
vague', which is not necessarily true. If Eliot and Auden
each show a high percentage of definite articles, their reasons
for doing so are fundamentally different, even though Eliot
exercised a potent influence on the young Auden:

> But Eliot spoke the still unspoken word;
> For gasworks and dried tubers I forsook
> The clock at Grantchester, the English rook.
> ('Letter to Lord Byron', IV)

A line like 'The simple act of the confused will' (from
Poem XXVII in *Poems*, later 'The Question' in *Collected
Shorter Poems*, 1966), to which Hamilton draws attention,
seems to be directly imitated from lines in Eliot's exactly
contemporary *Ash Wednesday*, such as 'The vanished power
of the usual reign' or 'The infirm glory of the positive
hour'. But this syntactical formation is rare in Auden and
can be regarded as an early, unassimilated influence. In
Eliot the use of the definite article attempts, wistfully or
urgently, to affirm the possibility of shared experiences
and feelings recalled out of a fragmentary and chaotic
past:

> But only in time can the moment in the rose-garden,
> The moment in the arbour where the rain beat,
> The moment in the draughty church at smokefall
> Be remembered . . . .

The experiences thus recalled are personal but not remote
or esoteric, and they seek an echo in our own pasts. Auden,
by contrast, can present bafflingly private experiences in
a similar way, so that the attempt to participate either
recoils or leads one on to speculative fiction-making:

A choice was killed by every childish illness,
The boiling tears among the hothouse plants,
The rigid promise fractured in the garden,
    And the long aunts.
      (Poem XXI in *Look, Stranger!*; 'A Bride in
      the Thirties' in *Collected Shorter Poems*)

The effect is, as Hamilton disapprovingly remarks, 'as though an entire stranger were claiming our acquaintance'. More often, however, Auden's use of the definite article arises from his sense of reality as known and charted and intelligible, where all elements are potentially at least capable of classification. To quote Hamilton once more: 'We have seen the fondness of Eliot and Auden for the particular image, Eliot lighting up the fragments of what is, or is supposed to be, our common experience, while Auden indicates the marks by which we may recognise this or that type of person, and diagnose his disease.' Auden's classifying tendency was familiar to his friends from the beginning. In Christopher Isherwood's *Lions and Shadows*, where the young Auden appears as 'Weston', the narrator thinks, on a seaside holiday, 'Suppose Weston were here . . . he would know the names of the different species of gull—and, by naming them, would dismiss them to the proper recognized unimportant place in the background of the poet's consciousness . . . .'

Another stylistic feature which Auden derived from Eliot but used with a significant difference is the bizarre or unexpected simile, as in the famous opening of 'Prufrock': 'When the evening is spread out against the sky / Like a patient etherised upon a table'. In Eliot the simile is startling but not unintelligible; the underlying idea is of the cessation of consciousness, and we are invited to recognise the strangeness of a sensibility that interprets common experience in such a clinical way. There is, too, the conviction of the early modernist poet that we should think and feel differently about such a hallowed Romantic property as 'evening'. In Auden this impulse is systematically taken to the point of diminishing, even trivialising, large, potent

concepts or images by comparing them to something everyday or banal. One example is 'Desire like a police-dog
is unfastened' (Poem X, *Look, Stranger!*); another is the
treatment of the moon in Poem II of *Look, Stranger!*:

> Into the galleries she peers,
> And blankly as an orphan stares
> Upon the marvellous pictures.

In the revised version of this poem, 'A Summer Night',
the comparison is made even more reductive: 'And blankly
as a butcher stares'. This stylistic device became more
frequent as Auden developed during the thirties; it is rare
in *Poems*, moderately common in *Look, Stranger!* and a
repetitive trick in *Another Time* (1940). 'Brussels in Winter'
from the last volume is representative, with four similes
in fourteen lines: 'Wandering the cold streets tangled like
old string'; 'The winter holds them like the Opera'; 'Where
isolated windows glow like farms'; 'A phrase goes packed
with meaning like a van'. Such repetitions deaden whatever
startling impact the device might have; it was, however,
widely imitated, and became a major element in the collective Audenesque manner.

Equally influential was Auden's reliance on adjectives
and adjectival phrases. These are sometimes scientific or
clinical. But others—not all of them used frequently, but
with a particular tactical emphasis—are partly descriptive,
partly affective, with the exaggerated overtones of a familiar
register in English middle-class speech: 'wonderful', 'marvel-
lous', 'lovely', 'horrible', 'appalling', 'tremendous', 'ridiculous', 'doubtful', 'enormous', 'absurd'. When applied to
natural objects, or to unlikely human artefacts or institutions,
the effect, as with the similes, is reductive, suggesting that
there is nothing in reality that cannot be contained within
the conceptual and verbal confines of the poet's world
of discourse. The effect is similar to Weston's hypothetical
classifying of seagulls as described by Isherwood. The prevalence of this device was adversely discussed by Karl Shapiro
in *Essay on Rime*:

> the tyrannical epithet
> Relies upon the adjective to produce
> The image; and no serious construction
> In rime can build upon the modifier.
> However matched and well-met are the words
> In such a phrase, the end-product is loose.
> *The high thin rare continuous worship of*
> *The self-absorbed* is an example which
> Outside of Auden has become the craze.
> *The tigerish blazer and the dove-like shoe*
> Is obviously the prototype for those
> Who speak diffusedly of *the childish night,*
> *Meaningless children, the albino crow,*
> *The riding flesh,* and *the unmurdered rose.*[4]

Shapiro overstates his case when he claims that 'no serious construction ... can build upon the modifier'. A heavy reliance on adjectives and adjectival phrases was a noticeable feature of Yeats's mature style at its most impressive and one which certainly influenced Auden's own practice. It is sufficient to dip into Yeats's *Collected Poems* to find striking examples: 'Many ingenious lovely things are gone' ('Nineteen Hundred and Nineteen'); 'horrible green parrots', 'the mad abstract dark' ('On a Picture of a Black Centaur by Edmund Dulac'); 'That dolphin-torn, that gong-tormented sea' ('Byzantium'). And there are instances before the twentieth century; one of Matthew Arnold's most plangent lines achieves its effect entirely by an accumulation of adjectives, and is proto-Audenesque in its combination of the affective and the descriptive: 'The unplumbed, salt, estranging sea'. Shapiro also seems to have missed the point about 'The tigerish blazer and the dove-like shoe' (from Poem XXX of *Look, Stranger!*, 'August for the People'), where the epithets are less arbitrary than he assumed. There is something of a witty conceit in describing the striped blazer and white tennis-shoes of the English holiday-maker in this way.

Nevertheless, Shapiro's discussion in *Essay on Rime* provides a generally acute description of the Audenesque. He notes

Auden's increasing inclination towards personified abstractions:

> Auden at first
> Used the abstraction as a metaphor,
> Concretely and with humour, but the figure,
> Full of the serum of old melancholy,
> Distended in its shell and burst. Thereafter
> The capital letter moved across his lines
> As ponderously as German nouns . . . .[5]

Again, Poem XXX of *Look, Stranger!* offers examples, though here the personification has something of the vigour and homeliness of Langland:

> Greed showing shamelessly her naked money,
> And all Love's wondering eloquence debased
> To a collector's slang, Smartness in furs,
> And Beauty scratching miserably for food . . . .

Shapiro goes on to show how certain key words of Auden's were generally adopted in the thirties and early forties:

> Consider for instance the innocuous word,
> A common noun in this case, *history*;
> Though Auden keeps it such, by subtle change
> It gradually acquires the vast range
> Of signification of a word like *God*.
> Auden has written poems on *hell* and *law*
> But these thus far are innocent of corrupt
> Generalization; but *history* has achieved
> A currency in our rhetoric the like
> Of which I think must be unparalleled
> In rime. I won a wager once that opening
> A magazine of verse at random, one
> Could put his finger on this word, and used
> Moreover in some sense of mystery
> Which would defy interpretation. Surely
> An all-purpose abstraction is a form
> Dear to the tired mind that must malinger
> And precious to the talentless; how can

The imitator well resist the coin
Left over by the rich in art? Abused,
Misued and uglified a thousandfold,
The counter passes for the purest gold
From poem to poem, until by reputation
It has acquired the superstitious force
Of the highbrow password. *History* is but one
Of Auden's ill-starred words. *Luck* is another.[6]

Others, one might add, are 'Love' and 'Europe', though
'History' was peculiarly obtrusive and influential. There
is a striking antecedent in Eliot's 'Gerontion', where 'History
has many cunning passages, contrived corridors'. In Auden's
own poetry it occurs in rhetorically significant places rather
than with great statistical frequency. One instance is in
the final lines of Poem **XXX** from *Look, Stranger!*:

And all sway forward on the dangerous flood
Of history, that never sleeps or dies,
And, held one moment, burns the hand.

Another is in the celebrated conclusion of 'Spain', which
Auden later came to regard with abhorrence: 'History to
the defeated / May say Alas but cannot help or pardon.'
As a concept, 'History' has obvious Marxist implications,
but as used in this personified way may have been suggested
to Auden by Edward Upward. Upward's story 'Sunday'
was written as early as 1931 and first published in *New
Country* in 1933 together with Auden's poems. This didactic
Marxist fable presents 'History' as a recurring personification, with a characteristic listing of disparate items:

History is here in the park, in the town. It is in the
offices, the duplicators, the traffic, the nursemaids wheeling
prams, the airmen, the aviary, the new viaduct over
the valley. It was once in the castle on the cliff, in
the sooty churches, in your mind; but it is abandoning
them, leaving with them only the failing energy of desper-
ation, going to live elsewhere.[7]

Upward seems to have been long preoccupied by 'History'.
In *Lions and Shadows* Isherwood quotes a letter from
'Chalmers' as a Cambridge undergraduate: 'Beware of the
daemon of history: it is merciless, it casually eats the flesh
and heart and leaves the bleaching bones. History, history,
hysteria.'

In addition to Auden's use of the personified abstraction,
sometimes given emphasis by the use of a possessive, as
in 'And love's best glasses reach / No fields but are his
own', one can note his use of the vocative—'O love, the
interest itself in thoughtless Heaven'—and of phrases in
apposition, like 'New styles of architecture, a change of
heart', both noticeable features of the Audenesque. In the
1930 *Poems* we find Auden experimenting with an elliptical,
'telegraphese' manner, by omission of the definite article.
This characteristic is at the opposite pole to what became
Auden's normal practice, but, as G. Rostrevor Hamilton remarked, 'it is clear that Auden is *the*-conscious, and that, in
playing with the English language, he often deliberately
avoids the article, elsewhere so profuse in his work'. In
fact, the articleless manner became less noticeable after the
1930 volume. It was extensively used by Cecil Day Lewis
in *The Magnetic Mountain*, and occurs in Spender's poetry.
But it was not widely imitated. In general the characteristics
of the Audenesque in syntax and diction seem to me to
be those described above: copious use of the definite article;
unusual adjectives and adjectival phrases, and surprising
similes, which have a reductive or trivialising effect; and
personified abstractions. These features are functions of
Auden's imaginative universe, which regarded reality as
actually or potentially known and intelligible, without mys-
teries or uncertainty. Experience could be reduced to classifi-
able elements, as a necessary preliminary to diagnosis and
prescription. It is in terms of this predisposition that Auden's
early allegiance to Marxism and psychoanalysis can best
be understood; both were attractive as techniques of explanation. Unifying all stylistic elements, and much less easily
imitated, was Auden's characteristic tone, of calm certainty
and total self-confidence. The opening of 'Let History Be
My Judge' is representative:

We made all possible preparations,
Drew up a list of firms,
Constantly revised our calculations
And allotted the farms . . . .

Lists and catalogues were a noticeable feature of Auden's
world of intelligible extension, and so were maps and landscapes, not just as content but as structural elements. There
is an apposite stanza in Part IV of 'Letter to Lord Byron':

The part can stand as symbol for the whole:
  So ruminating in these last few weeks,
I see the map of all my youth unroll,
  The mental mountains and the psychic creeks,
  The towns of which the master never speaks,
The various parishes and what they voted for,
The colonies, their size, and what they're noted for.

I would argue that Auden's best early poetry, where his
feelings were most deeply engaged, has a geographical or
topographical structure. This is apparent in the airman's
eye-view of 'Consider' in *Poems* and throughout *The Orators*
(1932). John Fuller has suggested that Auden was influenced
in his panoramic visions by Hardy's *The Dynasts*, but the
possibility that he was also inspired by the actual experience
of looking at the country from an aeroplane should not
be discounted. There is a significant passage in Evelyn
Waugh's *Vile Bodies* (1930) which describes such a view,
presenting much of the familiar content of Audenesque
poetry:

Nina looked down and saw inclined at an odd angle
a horizon of straggling red suburb; arterial roads dotted
with little cars; factories, some of them working, others
empty and decaying; a disused canal; some distant hills
sown with bungalows; wireless masts and overhead power
cables; men and women were indiscernible except as
tiny spots; they were marrying and shopping and making
money and having children. The scene lurched and tilted

again as the aeroplane struck a current of air.   (Ch.
12)

In *Look, Stranger!*, which I take to be Auden's finest collec-
tion, there are several brilliant poems which combine a
sweeping topographical vision and calm, assured movement.
In some the vision is conceptual and map-like, in others
it embodies Auden's devotion to certain English landscapes,
usually of the Midlands and North, but also the Isle of
Wight, a favoured resort of Auden, Isherwood and Upward.
(Some of the best of these poems, like 'August for the
People', were, perversely, excluded from the *Collected Shorter
Poems*.) Written at about the same time is the justly celebrated 'Night Mail', originally a commentary for a documen-
tary film about the Post Office. Here, too, we see a precise
and affectionate sense of place, together with a witty list
of the contents of the Night Mail:

Letters with holiday snaps to enlarge in,
Letters with faces scrawled in the margin,
Letters from uncles, cousins and aunts,
Letters to Scotland from the South of France,
Letters of condolence to Highlands and Lowlands . . . .

To my mind the most beautiful of all these revelations
of the deep structure of Auden's imaginative world is the
opening chorus of the verse play he wrote with Christopher
Isherwood, *The Dog Beneath the Skin* (1935). All the qualities
are here: the sense of a wide geographical context, narrowing
down to a particular place; the listing of names as in
a gazetteer; and the relaxed yet strong and flowing movement
of the verse:

The Summer holds: upon its glittering lake
Lie Europe and the islands; many rivers
Wrinkling its surface like a ploughman's palm.
Under the bellies of the grazing horses
On the far side of posts and bridges
The vigorous shadows dwindle; nothing wavers.
Calm at this moment the Dutch sea so shallow

That sunk St. Pauls would ever show its golden cross
And still the deep water that divides us still from Norway.
We would show you at first an English village: You shall
    choose its location.
Wherever your heart directs you most longingly to look;
    you are loving towards it:
Whether north to Scots Gap and Bellingham where the
    black rams defy the panting engine:
Or west to the Welsh Marches; to the lilting speech and
    the magicians' faces:
Wherever you were a child or had your first affair
There it stands amidst your darling scenery:
A parish bounded by the wreckers' cliff; or meadows where
    browse the Shorthorn and the maplike Frisian
As at Trent Junction where the Soar comes gliding; out
    of green Leicestershire to swell the ampler current.

II

The central paradox about the Audenesque is that, although
by the end of the thirties it was disseminated throughout
the English-speaking world, and can be called a collective
style, its origins lay in one man's very personal, even idiosyncratic vision of reality. As, indeed, Shapiro acknowledged:

> The personal development of an English poet
> Became almost immediately the folly
> Of all who wrote in verse.[8]

If Auden was widely and rapidly imitated, at least in
his most evidently imitable stylistic and structural devices,
it was, I believe, because there was a general readiness
to look at the world in Auden's categories. At a time
of world economic depression there was something reassuring
in Auden's calm demonstration, mediated as much by style
as by content, that reality was intelligible, and could be
studied like a map or a catalogue, or seen in temporal
terms as an inexorable historical process. Hence the instant
appeal of the classificatory vision, the reliance on definite

articles and precise if unexpected adjectives, which placed
and limited their subjects. Indeed, Auden's view of things
was in a sense already in the air, as in the general admiration
for the supposed virtues of the Soviet Five-Year Plan. If
Auden liked lists, so too did the practitioners of that primitive
kind of sociological enquiry called 'Mass Observation', which
tried to understand social behaviour by accumulating disparate observations about what given groups of people were
doing at any one time. 'Mass Observation' was sponsored
by a poet and sociologist, Charles Madge, and its activities
were sympathetically described in *New Verse*. One may
compare the title of Geoffrey Grigson's first book of poems,
Several Observations (1939); some of the early poems of Grigson
and Kenneth Allott make use of lists in a way that recalls
sociological investigation as well as Auden's models. There
is a curious example in Kenneth Allott's 'Signs', published
in *New Verse* in 1936:

> the letter to write
> the seaside cruet
> the magic flute
>
> goldbearing quartz
> the speeding fox
> the last waltz
>
> the rising gale
> the flowered voile
> the schoolbell . . .
>
> the flying start
> the dish-clout
> the murdered heart.

There are other possible sources for this manner, quite
independent of Auden's poetic practice: some of the most
famous and enduring popular songs of the thirties, for
instance, like 'You're the Top' and 'These Foolish Things',
were made up of lists of random items.

By 1936, when the Spanish Civil War broke out, the

Audenesque had become an established idiom, as we see
in 'Full Moon at Tierz: Before the Storming of Huesca',
written by the young Communist poet John Cornford not
long before his death in Spain. The first section contains
the almost obligatory reference to 'history':

> And history forming in our hand's
> Not plasticine but roaring sands,
> Yet we must swing it to its final course.

The final section opens with a remarkably assured example
of the Audenesque, with the characteristic geographical
sweep, the reductive adjectives, the personifications, and
the use of the vocative. It is nicely sustained for two
stanzas, but in the third Cornford shifts into a more directly
hortatory manner:

> Now the same night falls over Germany
> And the impartial beauty of the stars
> Lights from the unfeeling sky
> Oranienburg and freedom's crooked scars.
> We can do nothing to ease that pain
> But prove the agony was not in vain.
>
> England is silent under the same moon,
> From the Clydeside to the gutted pits of Wales.
> The innocent mask conceals that soon
> Here, too, our freedom's swaying in the scales.
> O understand before too late
> Freedom was never held without a fight.
>
> Freedom is an easily spoken word
> But facts are stubborn things. Here, too, in Spain
> Our fight's not won till the workers of all the world
> Stand by our guard on Huesca's plain
> Swear that our dead fought not in vain,
> Raise the red flag triumphantly
> For Communism and for liberty.[9]

The most famous poem to emerge from the Spanish Civil

War, and one which seems to me the apogee of the Audenesque, was Auden's own 'Spain'. First published as a pamphlet
in 1937, it was reprinted in a revised form in *Another
Time*, but was finally dropped from the *Collected Shorter
Poems*. Among other things, 'Spain' is a catalogue poem
where, as G. Rostrevor Hamilton showed, the percentage
of definite articles is no less than 20 per cent. Hamilton
was altogether too dismissive about 'Spain', calling it 'a
succession of calculated phrases without any backbone of
verbs: the degeneration of syntax'. Despite its accumulative
method the poem does have, as C. K. Stead has pointed
out,[10] a coherent structure, with the form 'Yesterday all
the past' / 'Tomorrow perhaps' / 'But today the struggle'.

In 'Spain' the geographical images are no longer the
occasion of dispassionate surveys; the map has become the
location for a violent, cataclysmic struggle:

On that arid square, that fragment nipped off from hot
Africa, soldered so crudely to inventive Europe,
      On that tableland scored by rivers,
Our fever's menacing shapes are precise and alive.

'Spain' is an immensely interesting poem, where Auden
tries to meet a new and urgent situation with a method
that was more suited to the calm analysis and diagnosis
of historical and social disorder than to facing so immediate
a challenge. It has given rise to arguments about the
nature of political poetry, and about such particular conten-
tious points as the phrase, later amended, 'the conscious
acceptance of guilt in the necessary murder'.[11] But in the
end the interest seems to me more historical than literary,
despite C. K. Stead's careful advocacy of the poem's merits.
For all its local brilliance 'Spain' looks strained and unconvincing and, perhaps, unconvinced; I find it a lesser achievement than many of the poems that Auden wrote earlier
in the decade. Most significantly, 'Spain' shows signs of
self-imitation, of Auden becoming self-conscious in his
employment of the Audenesque, possibly by feedback from
his imitators.

Certainly 'Spain' gave a powerful boost to the development of the Audenesque in the late thirties, particularly in the portentous references to 'History'. Auden himself continued to write in the familiar idiom but, as some of the poems in *Another Time* indicate, in an increasingly insensitive manner. After his removal to America he adopted other voices and styles, with the protean ease that had always been characteristic of him. But it was not yet the end of the Audenesque chapter in English poetry.

III

Julian Symons has remarked that in the early thirties English culture was polarised between ideas of catastrophe and ideas of rebirth.[12] This polarity is evident in the poetry of Auden and his disciples, where images of derelict mills and factories and rusty sidings are set against others of pylons and aeroplanes and 'new styles of architecture'; economic and industrial collapse contrasting with revolutionary hopes for the future, whether political or technological. The Audenesque, as a manner adapted to typification and analysis, enacted this polarity. The poet was like an aerial observer studying a landscape, pointing to disaster areas here and there, but also pointing elsewhere to new centres of civic and industrial growth. The advent of war, first in Spain in 1936 and then in the rest of Europe in 1939, destroyed this polarity. Catastrophe was present and total and the possibility of rebirth seemed more and more remote. After the outbreak of the Second World War and Auden's departure from England the Audenesque seemed to have lost its *raison d'être*. This, indeed, is a common assumption of literary history, where the 'social realist' poetry of the thirties disappears and is replaced overnight by the 'neo-Romanticism' of the forties. If one looks at the poetry actually written during the Second World War the facts appear otherwise, for the Audenesque persisted, and servicemen or civilians found it an acceptable manner for the poetic registration of wartime experience. The implications of the style were, however, significantly altered. The use of definite articles and adjectives, instead of projecting a conceptual

map of the known and knowable, indicated a nightmare
landscape, or a concrete and detailed but alien and threatening environment. Again, references to 'History' were as
frequent as ever, but that entity was no longer a godlike
force inexorably directing the course of human development;
it seemed, now, the very embodiment of the irrational
and the destructive:

Now I ask love from the stars in a time of hate
And, also, beg peace from the voice of the dead.
I cannot, however much I desire it, deny the past.
What, I say to the midsummer moon, can I do in this
    city,
And where can I walk to avoid the lies of history?
                (Ruthven Todd, 'In Edinburgh 1940')

        Reader, could his limbs be found
        Here would lie a common man:
        History inflicts no wound
        But explodes what it began,
        And with its enormous lust
        For division splits the dust.
        (Roy Fuller, 'Epitaph on a Bombing Victim')

History rears before us like a wave,
Its high white head poised while we catch a breath,
While sun is torn from sky, and cowed or brave
We dare the disaster or the new adventure . . . .
            (Herbert Corby, 'Poem on Joining the Royal
            Air Force, 1941')

O love! is it worth it? And are the dead rewarded
With a bearer bond on history's doubtful balance?
And is the loss redeemed by a sunset glory
A sweet transfusion of blood to a new-born world?

No, it will never be worth it, nor the loss redeemed.

      (Randall Swingler, 'Briefing for Invasion')

The map, which in the thirties was a reassuring image
of order and coherence, acquired a deceptive or sinister
character:

> A map of the world is on the wall: its lying
> Order and compression shadow these bent heads.
> Here we try to preserve communications;
> The map mocks us with dangerous blues and reds.
>   (Roy Fuller, 'Y.M.C.A. Writing Room')

> Time may have answers but the map is here.
> Now is the future that I never wished to see.
> I was quite happy dreaming and had no fear:
> But now, from the map, a gun is aimed at me.
>   (Ruthven Todd, 'It was Easier')

Keith Douglas directed the Audenesque airman's eye-view
at a desert battlefield:

> Perched on a great fall of air
> a pilot or angel looking down
> on some eccentric chart, the plain
> dotted with the useless furniture
> discerns crouching on the sand vehicles
> squashed dead or still entire, stunned
> like beetles: scattered wingcases and
> legs, heads, show when the haze settles.
>   ('Landscape with Figures')

In 'The Middle of a War', Roy Fuller provides a memorable
Audenesque line that deflates a large historical vision with
a reductive adjective and simile: 'The ridiculous empires
break like biscuits'.

The wartime persistence of the Audenesque was inevitably
tenuous, since it was a manner sustained at two removes
from its source. It was a continuation, in totally changed
circumstances, of the collective idiom of the thirties, itself
incorporating the personal mannerisms of one poet. Yet
the Audenesque was still viable by the end of the war,
as we see from an early poem by a writer who was later
to become a dominant presence on the post-war literary

scene:

> Then if history had a choice, he would point his cameras
> Oh yes anywhere but here, any time but now;
> But this is given us as the end of something
> Important, something we must try to remember;
> No music or kisses we want attend the fade-out,
> Only a same sky or an embarrassing room,
> Lust for something and a lust for no one,
> Aloneness of crowds, infidelity, love's torture.
>   (Kingsley Amis, 'Belgian Winter')

Thereafter the Audenesque faded, though some of its stylistic features—particularly the extensive use of definite articles, and arresting adjectives and similes—were absorbed into the diction or syntax of later poets. What became quite inaccessible were those characteristics that were closest to Auden's own early vision of reality, the calm, confident, categorising manner, and the capacity for assured generalisation expressing itself in terms of history or geography. By the early fifties it had all come to seem very remote:

>   The Devil for a joke
>   Might carve his own initials on our desk,
>   And yet we'd miss the point because he spoke
>   An idiom too dated, Audenesque.
>   (Donald Davie, 'Remembering the Thirties')

But what looks merely dated after twenty years can be worth serious historical enquiry after forty years. One significant aspect of the triumph of the Audenesque in the late thirties is now apparent. It was the last time that any British poet was to have such a global influence on poetry in English. Thereafter the course of British and American poetry diverged sharply, so that now, as is often remarked, there are two quite separate poetic traditions with nothing in common. In a more theoretical way, a study of the Audenesque may contribute something to current discussions of the sociology of literature. It suggests that, whereas the study of stylistic changes in isolation from larger social and cultural factors is likely to be arid and unilluminating, simplistic attempts to relate literature and society are equally unhelpful. English critics and literary historians readily assume that a style spreads simply because an influential writer has imitators, but Continental theorists are inclined to regard style as an impersonal emanation of a 'world vision' or the spirit of the age. In my reading, both factors are necessary; Auden, as a very individual genius, devised, without intending to, a code in which other, less talented poets could express their fears and anxieties and hopes through a period of sustained historical crisis. If their messages are often remarkably similar, that is partly, no doubt, because of the conditioning nature of the code, and partly because of the collective nature of their preoccupations.

3 Auden/Greene

The advertisements trailed along the arterial road:
Bungalows and a broken farm, short chalky grass
Where a hoarding had been pulled down,
A windmill offering tea and lemonade,
The great ruined sails gaping.

Here, it seems, we have a run-of-the-mill piece of thirties
verse, Audenesque in style and subject. It shows a familiar
social knowingness, contrasting the new and the old, modernity and decay. The new is represented by the advertisements, the bungalows, and, in particular, the arterial road,
which as an emblem of the new technology recurs in poems
by Auden ('Escaping humming down arterial roads', in
'Consider'), Day Lewis ('Down arterial roads riding in
April', in *The Magnetic Mountain*, XXXII), and Bernard
Spencer ('Stare down the polished arterial road', in 'Suburb
Factories'). The Appendix to the *Oxford English Dictionary*
records a contracted use of 'arterial' as a substantive in
Harold Nicolson's *Some People* (1932): 'Jane Campbell . . .
sped along the Kent arterial.' Set against this modernity
are the signs of agricultural depression and a collapsing
rural order, the 'broken farm' being reminiscent of Orwell's
poem 'On a Ruined Farm near the His. Master's Voice
Gramophone Factory', or another line from Part XXXII
of *The Magnetic Mountain*: 'Yet passing derelict mills and
barns roof-rent'. The once-imposing windmill is now reduced
to serving refreshments to trippers. Stylistically, too, the
provenance of the lines is unmistakable. There is the use

of definite articles implying a known and recognised landscape, and a string of phrases in apposition, each presenting
a separate observation. (Only the grammatical tense is
a little surprising: most emblematically descriptive poetry
of this kind uses the present tense.) The diction, too, in
the portentous use of 'ruined' rather than 'broken' or
'damaged' is Audenesque. And there is a faint but clear
syntactical echo of one of Auden's constructions, if we
compare a phrase from these lines ('short chalky grass/
Where a hoarding had been pulled down') with one from
Auden's 'Consider' ('the silent comb / Where dogs have
worried, or a bird was shot').

The lines are not, however, from any poem of the period.
They are taken from Graham Greene's *Brighton Rock* (Part
V, ch. 1) and set out as verse. They reveal not just Greene's
capacity to pick up a prevalent tone and mode of observation, but the extent to which his fictional prose was affected
by Auden. There are many examples in *Brighton Rock* of
phrases that read, in isolation, like quintessentially Audenesque lines: 'the kind word in season to the despairing school-
girl in the Strand', occurring randomly in Ida Arnold's
ruminations, has the combined specificity and privacy that
we find so often in Auden's poetry; while Pinkie's consciousness, not long before his violent end, produces 'the cold
unhappy moment on the pier'. Such instances provide concrete demonstration of the high regard for Auden that
Greene expressed in his contribution to the 'Auden Special
Number' of *New Verse* in November 1937. There Greene
wrote, 'No room for criticism, only for the personal statement—that to me Mr. Auden is a long way the finest
living poet ... with the exception of *The Tower*, no volume
of poetry has given me more excitement than *Look,
Stranger!*' Already, in a film review in 1936, Greene had
referred to the 'Audenesque charm' of Cole Porter's 'You're
the Top'.[1] For novelists to be influenced by other novelists
is commonplace; but for a novelist to be influenced by
a poet is, on the face of it, rare. It is true that Auden's
style was particularly infectious, and his confident, generalis-
ing, typifying cast of mind offered what the age demanded.
His influence on poets spread widely and rapidly; nor,

indeed, was Greene the first novelist to be affected. The
following passage from Isherwood's *The Memorial* looks distinctly Audenesque in its use of definite articles and adjectival
classifying:

> The thin, delicate, staccato Frenchmen fiddling nervously
> with their cigarettes, winding themselves up slowly like
> springs while the others talked, then pouncing into a
> half second's opening in the conversation with their:
> '*Je suppose que.*' The small, untidy, worried-looking
> Spaniards, sombre and tragic, yet somehow like hair-
> dressers. The large, lazy Russians with many wives[2]

(though Edward Upward may have been equally influential). Yet there was more in Greene's attitude to Auden
than quickness to pick up a prevalent idiom. I believe
the affinities went deeper. If a highly gifted writer allows
himself to be heavily influenced, for a time, by another
writer, it is because the one who influences him provides
some necessary constituent to his art, by striking a sympathetic chord or unlocking a potentiality. Greene has recorded
how he was influenced in this way by Joseph Conrad,
excessively so in fact, so that for many years he refused
to read Conrad at all. Auden seems to have had a similar
effect on Greene in the thirties. There were evident similari-
ties between them. Both writers combined two quite disparate qualities: a private, idiosyncratic, even obsessional aspect,
often looking back to childhood or adolescent experience;
and a keen, observant, classifying interest in contemporary
mass society. Greene may well have found in Auden a
possible model for relating these aspects of his art. Both
writers were inclined to the categorising overview, which,
as I have argued, provided a rationale for the Audenesque
as a stylistic mode. As I have also remarked, Auden constantly and effectively used images and frames of reference
drawn from maps and geography; and so did Greene.
In his first canonical novel about the modern world, *Stamboul
Train*, the Orient Express steams across the map of Europe;
while his next novel and his two travel books of the thirties
all have titles with topographical implications: *It's a Battle-*

field; *Journey Without Maps*; *The Lawless Roads*. And on occasion Greene matches Auden's frequent metaphorical references to maps, as in *Brighton Rock*, where Rose's face is extravagantly referred to as 'like the map of a campaign marked with flags'.

Richard Hoggart, a critic who has written interestingly about both Auden and Greene, has noted the affinity between them, particularly in their taste for lists and catalogues:

> Greene uses the selectively typical catalogue as much as Auden, partly because they naturally tend to handle their material similarly, partly because they both began to write in the Thirties when reportage made the catalogue very popular. More importantly, it seems to me, Greene's use of the catalogue follows from his way of looking at life. If life is seen as a vast pattern then all the details of life can easily become part of the pattern; they can be 'placed' with a certain sureness and inevitability.[3]

This is surely as true of Auden's poetry as of Greene's fiction. Greene's use of the bizarre or arresting simile may also derive from Auden. Hoggart isolates a number of examples, which show Greene's art at its most characteristic and vulnerable. Like Auden's similes, they often relate the abstract and general to the specific and everyday or trivial: 'Evil ran like malaria in his veins', 'Heat stood in the room like an enemy', 'The old life peeled away like a label', 'He could feel his prayers weigh him down like undigested food'. It is possible, though, that both Auden and Greene had a common source and inspiration in the startling similes of the early Eliot, where 'The evening is spread out against the sky / Like a patient etherised upon a table', and 'Midnight shakes the memory / As a madman shakes a dead geranium'. Yet, whatever the derivation, for both Auden and Greene the simile was a means of instantly juxtaposing the particular and the general; and, as Hoggart remarks, such juxtapositions can function as allegory. Significantly, Auden, in an admiring note on

Greene, has applauded the way in which his thrillers have
an allegorical dimension.[4] Both writers had an inclination
towards allegory in their work of the thirties, even though
in Greene, as a novelist, the descriptive realism is necessarily
more prolonged and extensive.

What one can briefly if too simply call Greene's Audenesque phase largely coincided with his pre-war fiction, the
period of his late twenties and early thirties, when, though
a prolific writer of novels and 'entertainments', he was
still learning the craft of fiction, and was ready to make
use of whatever literary models he found helpful. His material was mostly English and urban, and he treated it in
the manner of the time, bringing together reportorial alert-
ness to significant cultural detail and a sense of mass society
as a large, complex, impersonal force. Greene seems to
know how it all fits together, even though his paradigm
is an idiosyncratic Catholic one, based in a polarity between
salvation and damnation, rather than the Marxist model
that was, for a time, favoured by Auden and his followers.
But the difference in ideology hardly affects the quality
of the observation, or the stylistic and formal modes of
categorising it. With *The Power and the Glory* in 1940, Greene's
art altered. There was less of the restless, ranging view
of urban society, since the action was now removed from
England to remote but spiritually authentic parts of the
globe, and the emphasis was more emphatically on the
human dramas being enacted in the foreground. The style,
too, eventually became subdued and chastened, less extravagant in its metaphors and similes. The Audenesque was
phased out, though Greene could still slip into it again,
as he does in his one substantial post-war novel with
an English setting, *The End of the Affair* (1951). In most
respects it is unlike Greene's novels of the thirties, with
no social categorising or exact, cinematic detail. Yet, in
the third chapter, in which the narrator, Maurice Bendrix,
is looking back to 1939, we find the following, which
I have once more arranged as verse, like the earlier passage
from *Brighton Rock*:[5]

How can I disinter
The human character from the heavy scene—

The daily newspaper, the daily meal,
The traffic grinding towards Battersea,
The gulls coming up from the Thames looking for
  bread,
And the early summer of 1939
Glinting on the park where the children sailed
  their boats—
One of those bright condemned pre-war summers?

The last line is purely Audenesque, as it sums up the
preceding list of disparate observations; there is the confident
placing use of the demonstrative, and the calculated lexical
clash of the adjectives; it recalls, if it does not echo, the
first line of Auden's 'In Memory of Ernst Toller'—'The
shining neutral summer has no voice'—itself written in
the summer of 1939. Recalling the period, it seems, meant
recalling the style.

4 Transformations of the Frontier

In Christopher Isherwood's *Mr Norris Changes Trains* (1935) his eponymous hero complains in the opening chapter, 'All these frontiers ... such a horrible nuisance.' It is a remark with a resonance far beyond the immediate context. In the literature of the 1930s the frontier is an insistent element, whether as literal description or emblem or symbol. In W. H. Auden's first collection, the diminutive, privately printed (by Stephen Spender) *Poems* of 1928, Poem V begins,

> On the frontier at dawn getting down,
> Hot eyes were soothed with swallows: ploughs began
> Upon the stunted ridge behind the town,
> And bridles flashed.

Auden did not reprint this poem, but ten years later the phrase 'on the frontier' provided the title for the last of the verse plays that he wrote in collaboration with Isherwood. The frontier was an aspect of a subjective and inner landscape in the poetry of Auden and his imitators: a metaphorical division between states of feeling, between known and unknown, present and future, the small group and society. The image was precise, but its implications were very general and capable of almost endless extension. It occurs in Poem XVIII of the 1930 *Poems* (later called 'This Loved One'), which was written about a German boy that Isherwood was in love with in Berlin.

> Before this last one
> Was much to be done,
> Frontiers to cross
> As clothes grew worse
> And coins to pass
> In a cheaper house
> Before this last one
> Before this loved one.

And in Poem III (later 'Venus Will Now Say a Few Words') Auden writes in his characteristically cryptic but imperative manner

> Do not imagine you can abdicate;
> Before you reach the frontier you are caught;
> Others have tried it and will try again
> To finish that which they did not begin . . . .

In *The Orators* of 1932 Auden rewrites his line of 1928 in the prose 'Argument': 'At the frontier getting down, at railhead drinking hot tea waiting for pack-mules, at the box with the three levers watching the swallows. Choosing of guides for the passage through gorges.' In Ode V of *The Orators* (which became the Ode IV in the third edition of 1956 and 'Ode' in *Collected Shorter Poems*) Auden presents his most extended treatment of the frontier. This poem is vigorous in language and movement, but desperately obscure; the setting is Auden's favoured mountainous northern landscape, vivid but non-specific, so that it can seem in places Icelandic or Scandinavian, in other places Pennine, with abandoned industrial installations. The situation suggests some kind of undeclared war, perhaps with guerrilla skirmishings across a frontier, in an amplification of the feuds in 'Paid on Both Sides'. The intention is metaphorical but the local detail is sharply rendered:

> They speak of things done on the frontier we were
>   never told,
> They will never reveal though kept without sleep,
>   for their code is

'Death to the squealer':
They are brave, yes, though our newspapers mention
   their bravery
            In inverted commas.

But careful; back to our lines; it is unsafe there,
Passports are issued no longer; that area is closed;
There's no fire in the waiting-room now at the
   climber's Junction,
            And all this year
Work has been stopped on the power-house; the wind
   whistles under
            The half-built culverts.

Cecil Day Lewis, Auden's most sedulous disciple, was quick
to introduce frontiers into his poetry. In Part XV of *From
Feathers to Iron* (1931) he writes,

   I have come so far upon my journey.
   This is the frontier, this is where I change,
   And wait between two worlds to take refreshment

and in Part XXVII of the same poem,

      Is fighting on the frontier: little leaks through
      Of possible disaster, but one morning
      Shells begin to drop in the capital.

In *The Magnetic Mountain* (1933), Part II, 7, Day Lewis
uses the frontier to indicate a change of consciousness:

         Simply, one day
      He crossed the frontier and I did not follow:
      Returning, spoke another language.

In 1932 John Cornford, then a schoolboy of sixteen, closely
echoed Auden and Day Lewis:

      At the street corners they were selling papers
      Told us what teeth were broken in what riots,

Where fighting on the frontier is unsuccessful
But causes as yet no panic in the city.
Think. Rome felt not otherwise than this
Who, dying slowly, is spared defeat,
Suffers, perhaps, greater humiliation.
　　　　('At least to know the sun rising each morning',
　　　　in *Understand the Weapon*, p. 26)

(Within a few years, Cornford's fate led him across a
frontier, to die fighting in Spain in 1936.) In *New Country*
the idea is becoming a commonplace (the very idea of
a 'new country' implies a frontier). John Lehmann there
writes in his Poem III, 'but in the Spring he plans / Walking
beside a friend to cross the frontier', while Richard Goodman
begins his thinly Audenesque 'Ode to a Dead Comrade'
with the stanza:

　　　　Comrade, the sun today
　　　　that stands erect with joy,
　now Autumn swings it to a stricter course,
　　　　no sorrow will admit
　　　　and we, in step with it,
　come to new frontiers, cancel out remorse.

The same poet contributes 'The Squadrons', a neo-Futurist
praise of aeroplanes as a symbol of the coming world
revolution which will abolish frontiers:

　　　　dark towns float out beneath them at their will
　　　　and, cancelled in the avalanche of light,
　　　　the scribbled frontiers vanish from the map
　　　　until,
　　　　like flower, the world-state whirls across their
　　　　　　sight.

In *The Thirties: A Dream Revolved* Julian Symons remarks,
with particular reference to Auden, Isherwood and Edward
Upward, 'a predominant image for all these writers is
that of the frontier'. His explanatory comment is pertinent
as far as it goes, but it seriously understates the importance

of the frontier as a literary idea in the thirties:

> What fun everything is on this side of the frontier, how
> deliciously cosy it is to be with friends who talk one's
> own sort of serio-comic nonsense: yet on the other side
> life, as it seems, is going on. On the other side, the
> myth of the future: on ours, the myth of Mortmere.[1]

The frontier could indeed support that sense of enclosure
and exclusiveness: but as a category of experience it was
also part of the world of contemporary history and politics.

Whatever the appeal of the frontier as a flexible symbol,
the significance of which could be variously psychological,
social and political, one needs to remember that it derived
its basic force from the historical conditions of the twenties
and thirties. The peace treaties at the end of the First
World War, following the disappearance of the empires
of Central Europe, had multiplied the number of nation-
states and inscribed many more frontiers across the map.
And, whereas before 1914 the existing frontiers of Europe
had been only a formality, and could, for the most part,
be crossed without travel documents, the post-war frontiers
were formidable barriers. They implied passports and visas
and armed guards. As the thirties developed, the frontier
continued to be a potent idea for English writers, but
with a new dimension of observable reality; before long
the imaginary wars and insurrections projected by Auden
and Day Lewis and Cornford became matter-of-fact. One
sees the process beginning in Stephen Spender's *Vienna*,
a long poem published in 1934. No one, least of all its
author, has ever considered *Vienna* a successful poem, and
Spender has never allowed it to be reprinted. Yet, though
a poetic failure, it is an ambitious and instructive failure,
and Samuel Hynes has written a perceptive account of
it in *The Auden Generation*. The poem's genesis lay in the
bloody events in Austria in February 1934, when the workers'
militia of the Social Democratic party came into armed
conflict with the clerical–authoritarian (or 'Austro-fascist')
government of Dolfuss. The episode was variously described
as an attempt at a socialist revolution, a counter-revolution-

ary *coup*, or a short-lived civil war. The struggle ended
in disaster for the socialists, culminating in an event that
fired the imagination of the Left all over Europe, the
bombardment of the Vienna workers' flats, and notably
the Karl Marx Hof, by government artillery. Spender's
poem is an attempt to bring together this historical tragedy
and the disturbances of his inner life. He has described
in *World Within World* how, at that time, he was much
concerned with relating the public and the private dimensions of his own life, and he writes of *Vienna*,

> The most ambitious—and perhaps the least successful—
> attempt I made to solve the problem of making such
> a statement was in a longish poem called *Vienna* which
> I wrote in 1935 [published, in fact, in November 1934].
> In part this expressed my indignation at the suppression
> of the Viennese Socialists by Dolfuss, Fey and Stahrem-
> berg: but in part also it was concerned with a love
> relationship. I meant to show that the two experiences
> were different, yet related. For both were intense, emo-
> tional and personal, although the one was public, the
> other private. The validity of the one was dependent
> on that of the other: for in a world where humanity
> was trampled on publicly, private affection was also under-
> mined. The poem fails because it does not fuse the
> two halves of a split situation, and attain a unity where
> the inner passion becomes inseparable from the outer
> one.[2]

Vienna is an attempt by Spender to span the frontier between
the public and the private, and, as Samuel Hynes remarks,
perhaps only Yeats in our time has been able effectively
to relate the two worlds. But when, in Part III of the
poem, 'The Death of Heroes', Spender writes of a frontier,
he does so in a context of historical meaning referring
to attempts to escape by the defeated Austrian socialists.
His lines, though, read very like the imaginary frontier
references of Auden and his followers, and one notes the
presence of the word 'lucky', a characteristic piece of
Audenesque diction:

> Less lucky too
> Those who ran far like images of winds
> As cold as knives, eyeless and voiceless: heard
> Incredible flames, the sound of welcome: had
> Collapsing, reached the frontier. They related
> How they had lost. The desolate
> Praise mocks the defeated 'You're heroes'.

We see here a literary symbol, itself derived from new historical circumstance, being charged with particular significance. When, in the last section of *Vienna* (IV), Spender again uses the frontier, its significance, though the context still echoes the tragedy of February 1934, has become once more literary and general. Spender has retreated to familiar ground, invoking a stock salvation figure of the early thirties; in Mr Hynes's words, 'he imagines a stranger, another of those healing heroes who are central to the 'thirties myth, whose coming will drive out the sicknesses of the past'.[3]

> He greets the
> Historians of the future, the allies of no city,
> O man and woman minute beneath their larger day;
> Those burrowing beneath frontier, shot as spies
>   because
> Sensitive to new contours . . . .

For a year or so the defeat of February 1934 served as a forlorn symbol of socialist resistance to fascist encroachment. (Dolfuss himself was murdered by Austrian Nazis in July 1934.) Then, in July 1936, when the popular forces in Spain defeated the generals' insurrection in Madrid and Barcelona, the Left found new hope and a new instant mythology, and the ensuing civil war appeared as the ultimate polarity of Left and Right, democracy (as well as revolution) and fascism, hope and despair, life against death. Louis MacNeice, in Book VI of *Autumn Journal*, looked back to a visit he had made to Spain at Easter 1936:

And next day took the boat
  For home, forgetting Spain, not realising
That Spain would soon denote
  Our grief, our aspirations;
Not knowing that our blunt
  Ideals would find their whetstone, that our spirit
Would find its frontier on the Spanish front,
  Its body in a rag-tag army.

Henceforth the image of the frontier acquired a new and precise significance, indicated in the title, *Journey to the Frontier*, that William Abrahams and Peter Stansky gave to their book about two young Englishmen, Julian Bell and John Cornford, members of famous intellectual families, who died in the Spanish Civil War. The title alludes to literary works such as *On the Frontier* by Auden and Isherwood, and *Journey to the Border* by Edward Upward. But the journey was now actual and the frontier was real, lying between France and Republican Spain, across which volunteers poured from all over the world to fight for the Republic. As Auden wrote in 'Spain',

  They clung like birds to the long expresses that
    lurch
  Through the unjust lands, through the night, through
    the alpine tunnel;
      They floated over the oceans;
  They walked the passes. All presented their lives.

For the many visitors to Republican Spain who went as sympathisers or propagandists, crossing the frontier from France meant a transition to a new world of faith and hope and meaning. Cyril Connolly was one such, and in his essay 'Barcelona', dated November 1936, he wrote,

  The first thing one notices about going to Barcelona
  is the peculiar meaningful handshakes of one's friends.
  Accompanied though they are by some such phrase as
  'I wish I were going too', one cannot avoid detecting
  in the farewell a moment of undertaker heartiness, of

mortuary appraisal. In the early morning among the
lagoons, the brown landscape and rainy sky of Languedoc,
one begins to share it, only at the Spanish frontier does
it completely disappear. As a rule, the change from
Cerbère to Port Bou is one from gaiety and comfort
to gloom and emptiness; today it is the Spanish end
which is alive. The first thing one notices is the posters,
extremely competent propaganda, of which that of a
peasant's rope-soled foot descending on a cracked swastika
in a cobbled street is the most dramatic.[4]

One of Stephen Spender's best poems about the war in
Spain takes its name and setting from the Spanish frontier
town of Port Bou:

> A lorry halts beside me with creaking brakes
> And I look up at warm waving flag-like faces
> Of militiamen staring down at my French newspaper.
> 'How do they speak of our struggle over the
>   frontier?'

One of the very last British visitors to wartime Spain
was Louis MacNeice, who went there at the end of December
1938, when it was evident that the Spanish Republic had
lost the war. MacNeice gives an account of his visit to
embattled and half-starved Barcelona in Book XXIII of
Autumn Journal; but he wrote a fuller description in his
unfinished autobiography, *The Strings are False*. Despite the
now desperate situation of the Republic there is still a
sense of moving to a new world on entering from France:

> I hated Perpignan with its little canal-like river running
> between stunted trees, and was glad to leave again next
> morning, a beautiful candid day. At Le Perthus this
> time they approved my passport and allowed me a little
> further downhill, into actually Spanish territory. I was
> told to wait in a shed where a number of Basque soldiers
> were gathered round a small iron stove ... I walked
> around the shed looking at the political posters—Negrin's
> Thirteen Points, warnings against spies—a man with an

enormous ear or an enormous eye, a man with swastika
eyes and fasces for a nose.[5]

Later, driving to Barcelona, MacNeice reflects: 'I could
not believe where I was. "This is Spain," I said to myself.
"This is where war is." The signposts at the crossroads
said so many kilos to Madrid.'[6] MacNeice spent several
days in Barcelona, vividly recalled in *The Strings Are False*.
He left by air early in January 1939 and later that
month the Nationalist army of General Yagüe occupied
the city. Then the frontier acquired a new and grim significance, as thousands of Republican troops and civilians
poured across into France, to face internment and depriva-
tion and, in many cases, death from exposure or illness.
(Among those who perished was the poet Antonio Machado,
whom MacNeice had met in Barcelona).

Already, though, there had been refugees from Republican
Spain who were fleeing not the fascists but their own
side. Among the most notable was George Orwell. As he
describes in *Homage to Catalonia* (1938), he fought, not in
the Communist-supported International Brigades around
Madrid, but in the militia of the P. O. U. M. (*Partido
Obrero de Unificación Marxista*). In the spring of 1937 the
Republican Government, increasingly under the control of
the Communists, ruthlessly suppressed the revolutionary and
non-Communist Left. Orwell, on leave from the front in
Barcelona, was a horrified witness of the bitter street-fighting
there, the 'civil war within the civil war', which ended
in the defeat of the P. O. U. M. and the Anarchists. Orwell
returned to the front and was wounded in the throat,
almost fatally. Eventually, still not fully recovered from
his wound, he left hospital and was medically discharged
from the militia. On his return to Barcelona he found
that the P. O. U. M. had been denounced as 'fascist' and
that a full-scale persecution of its members was under way.
Orwell himself became a prime suspect. He describes both
the dangerous and the farcical aspects of his efforts to
escape the Republic's secret police. In the end, he and
his wife and another British suspect 'crossed the frontier
without incident', as he drily remarked. Much had changed

in the six months since Orwell had first crossed into Spain. Then, the Anarchists, full of revolutionary zeal, had been manning the frontier:

> And at the frontier the Anarchist guards had turned back a smartly dressed Frenchman and his wife, solely—I think—because they looked too bourgeois. Now it was the other way about; to look bourgeois was the one salvation. At the passport office they looked us up in the card-index of suspects, but thanks to the inefficiency of the police our names were not listed, not even McNair's. We were searched from head to foot, but we possessed nothing incriminating, except my discharge-papers, and the carabineros who searched me did not know that the 29th Division was the P. O. U. M. So we slipped through the barrier, and after just six months I was on French soil again.[7]

Orwell was one of the few Englishmen in the thirties who had undergone the experience of crossing a frontier as a wanted suspect.

II

In his writings of the thirties Graham Greene often used the idea or image of the frontier, but in such a personal way as to require separate, almost parenthetical treatment. His first novel to arouse much interest was *Stamboul Train* of 1932—*Orient Express* in the American edition—which follows the fortunes and misadventures of passengers travelling across Europe in a glamorous international express. As Greene remarks in his preface in the Collected Edition, the novel was in some respects written according to the formula recently made fashionable by Vicki Baum's *Grand Hotel*: focusing on a very mixed group of people, brought temporarily and arbitrarily together by external circumstance. The 'train' version was popular in novels and films of the early thirties; in 1933 Agatha Christie published *Murder on the Orient Express*, which exploits the formula to the utmost. *Stamboul Train* was also filmed, though, as Greene recalls, the film version had to trail behind such productions as *Shanghai Express* (starring Dietrich), *Rome Express*, and the Russian *Turksib*. International expresses necessarily cross frontiers, and in *Stamboul Train* some of the action takes place at the Yugoslav frontier town of Subotica. It is a real place, but Greene had not been there when he wrote *Stamboul Train*. In the 1974 preface he explains that though he travelled on the Orient Express to collect impressions he could not afford to go further than Cologne, and had to rely on his imagination for the remainder of the journey. So this particular frontier is, in Greene's book, both real and imagined. In the novel, Dr Czinner, an exiled Yugoslav Communist is returning to his native country, where a revolution is expected. At the frontier Dr Czinner is apprehended by guards, and so is Coral Musker, an English chorus-girl, travelling to take up a job in Istanbul. Dr Czinner has attempted to pass a message to Coral; both are arrested, and held under guard on the station. Czinner is tried by a drum-head court martial, presided over by the Chief of Police, Colonel Hartrep. In the course of this mock trial Czinner calls out to Hartrep, 'How old-fashioned you are with your frontiers and your patriotism. The aeroplane doesn't know a frontier; even your financiers don't recognize frontiers.' (The idea that the marked increase of frontiers in Europe in fact coincided with their essential obsolescence recurs in the English writing of the early thirties.) After some suspenseful action Dr Czinner is shot while attempting to escape, and Coral is rescued by the sinister lesbian journalist Mabel Warren.

Stamboul Train is a readable though minor work, and interesting in a symptomatic way. Its treatment of the frontier is mediated both by the conventions of the popular thriller and by the political realities of contemporary Europe. One notes, though, that the exchange between Czinner and Hartrep looks forward to fuller debates between ideologically opposed protagonists in Greene's later fiction, particularly the Priest and the Lieutenant in *The Power and the Glory*. The political dimension of the novel is very hazy, but the muffled reports of a left-wing rising in Belgrade seem to anticipate, in what is perhaps a very early example of Greene's notable prescience in such matters, the events in Vienna in February 1934.

In 1936, following the visit to Liberia described in *Journey Without Maps*, Greene began work on a novel called 'The Other Side of The Border', a title characteristic both of the time (the *Left Review* published contributions called 'Across the Border' and 'On the Border') and of Greene's own preoccupations. The novel was shortly abandoned, but Greene included the unfinished fragment in his collection *Nineteen Stories* (1947), together with a prefatory note. In this note Greene says that he began the novel soon after his return from Africa: 'at any rate, if it has no other merit, the book seems to me stamped unmistakably with the atmosphere of the middle thirties—Hitler is quite new, dictatorship is only a tang on the breeze blowing from Europe: in England is depression and a kind of metroland culture'. Greene adds that he abandoned the novel because another book—*Brighton Rock*—'was more insistent to be written, and because I realised that I had already dealt with the main character in a story called *England Made Me*'. It appears that the 'border' of the title was between a British colony and an independent African nation, no doubt modelled on Liberia. The story opens with the prevalent Audenesque image of the 'map', but the style and imagery are insistently Conradian:

> The first thing young Morrow noticed in the waiting-room was the Map. There it hung where you would naturally expect it in the new offices of the New Syndicate, representing the coast, the rivers running in parallel black threads from the interior, the mountains feathered on the northern border and the forest a splash of dark green over everything—representing too to Morrow a whole obscure state of mind, a mystery from which he had at last escaped.

('Morrow' even echoes 'Marlow'.) A further reason for Greene to abandon 'The Other Side of the Border' may have been that he had not yet shaken off the Conrad influence that had been so dominant and unassimilated in *It's a Battlefield*. Greene seems, indeed, to have regretted his tentative resurrection of 'The Other Side of the Border', for he excluded the fragment when *Nineteen Stories* was enlarged to *Twenty-One Stories*, and it has never been reprinted.

Later in the thirties Greene made a more elaborate and personal treatment of the idea of being 'across the border'. I refer to the 'Prologue' of his travel book about Mexico, *The Lawless Roads* (1939). Here Greene skilfully uses the image of the frontier, by then a commonplace of literature and journalism, to refer both to a crucial aspect of his childhood, and to his actual situation at an international border, that between Mexico and the U.S.A. This 'Prologue' is at the same time one of Greene's most subjectively revealing and one of his most rhetorically calculated pieces of writing, showing his capacity to make the public and the private worlds serve as alternating metaphors for each other. He begins by recalling his own difficult situation when a schoolboy: the son of the headmaster of Berkhampstead School, living with the school boarders during the week, but rejoining his family at weekends. (Greene has since given a fuller account of his life then in his autobiography, *A Sort of Life*.)

> Two countries just here lay side by side. From the croquet lawn, from the raspberry canes, from the greenhouse and the tennis lawn you could always see—dominatingly— the great square Victorian buildings of garish brick: they looked down like skyscrapers on a small green countryside where the fruit trees grew and the rabbits munched. You had to step carefully: the border was close beside your gravel path.[8]

Greene elaborates the distinction between the two countries: the school, marked by austerity and cruelty, and his parents' home, civilised and kind—the two divided by only a green baize door. Greene sees the origin of much of his imaginative world and the obsessions that govern it in this strange, indeed unnatural, situation:

> One was an inhabitant of both countries: on Saturday
> and Sunday afternoons of one side of the baize door,
> the rest of the week of the other. How can life on
> a border be other than restless? You are pulled by
> different ties of hate and love. For hate is quite as
> powerful a tie: it demands allegiance. In the land of
> the skyscrapers, of stone stairs and cracked bells ringing
> early, one was aware of fear and hate, a kind of lawless-
> ness—appalling cruelties could be practised without a
> second thought; one met for the first time characters,
> adult and adolescent, who bore about them the genuine
> quality of evil. ... One escaped surreptitiously for an
> hour at a time: unknown to frontier guards, one stood
> at the wrong side of the border looking back . . . .[9]

Schooldays, like frontiers, were another major literary theme
of the thirties. Greene develops these carefully patterned
memories into a vivid but desperately bleak autobiographical
essay that describes his religious development and sets out
the themes of his early fiction. He also provides a rationale
for going to Mexico to investigate the persecution of religion
by a ferociously anti-clerical government. In Mexico, even
if it were a kind of hell, one might discover a more
authentic life than in the suburbanised Metroland around
Berkhampstead. Greene then devotes a page or two to
Mexico and the martyrdom of the Jesuit Father Pro in
1926, before returning to his opening image of a rabbit
on the croquet-lawn of his parents' house:

> The rabbits moved among the croquet hoops and a
> clock struck: God was there and might intervene before
> the music ended. The great brick buildings rose at the
> end of the lawn against the sky—like the hotels in the
> United States which you can watch from Mexico leaning
> among the stars across the international bridge.[10]

We turn the page to Chapter 1 of *The Lawless Roads*,
which is called 'The Border', and find that Greene's account

of crossing the international bridge from Texas to Mexico sounds as much like a metaphor as a physical experience:

> The border means more than a customs house, a passport officer, a man with a gun. Over there everything is going to be different; life is never again going to be quite the same after your passport has been stamped and you find yourself speechless among the money-changers. ... The atmosphere of the border—it is like starting over again; there is something about it like a good confession: poised for a few happy moments between sin and sin. When people die on the border they call it 'a happy death'.[11]

(Greene also gave fictional treatment to this particular border in a short story, 'Across the Bridge'.) *The Lawless Roads* is a magnificent travel book, but it does give the sense that, for all the hardships and real dangers Greene underwent, Mexico remains something of an inner landscape, a metaphor or objective correlative for his obsessions. But the experience was later given a larger imaginative form in *The Power and the Glory*. In that novel the priest ensures his death by voluntarily returning, on an errand of mercy, from a Mexican state where the practice of religion is tolerated to the one he has just left, where it is a capital offence. For many years the idea of life as a border between heaven and hell, salvation and damnation, whether expressed as a green baize door or a state border or an international frontier, was a major constituent of Greene's fiction.

III

Returning to the mainstream of English writing in the thirties, one finds historically real and critical frontiers. Christopher Isherwood's *Mr Norris Changes Trains* opens in a train approaching the frontier between Holland and Germany. His narrator, 'William Bradshaw', gets into conversation with his nervous travelling companion, Arthur Norris, who makes the remark quoted at the beginning of this chapter: 'All these frontiers ... such a horrible nuisance'. Norris is nervous because of his ludicrous and ineffectual activities as a secret agent. By the end of the novel the frontier has a more desperate importance. Hitler has come to power and is destroying the political opposition. Norris's young Communist friend, Otto, is on the run from the Nazis: 'Tomorrow he was going to leave Berlin. He'd try to work his way down to the Saar. Somebody had told him that was the easiest frontier to cross. It was dangerous, of course, but better than being cooped up here.' In 1937, William Empson, travelling to the Far East by train across Siberia, crossed another major international frontier, between the Soviet Union and China, and preserved the experience in a brief but pregnant poem, 'Manchouli', which begins,

> I find it normal, passing these great frontiers,
> That you scan the crowds in rags eagerly each
>   side . . . .

Actual frontiers, however, were less common a theme than metaphorical or symbolic frontiers. A typical instance of the latter occurs in the title Eric Ambler gave to the first of his distinguished spy thrillers, *The Dark Frontier* (1936). In Rex Warner's fable *The Wild Goose Chase* (1937), a frontier plays a prominent part. The book begins with a prologue, 'Far on Bicycles', of which this is the highly mannered opening paragraph:

> It seems, though it was many years ago, only yesterday that we citizens of a seaside town, standing in ranks along the esplanade, watched, cheering at the same time with all the force of our lungs, the outset of the three brothers who, with the inconsiderate fine daring of youth, were prepared, each in his own way, to go far on bicycles, distinguishing our town by an attempt which even the brothers only dimly understood and which seemed to most of us who stood spectators vociferously cheering impracticable, to some even ridiculous. Young and vigorous they looked, different one from the other, as

they wheeled into the square their diverse coloured bicycles, made by the same maker at different dates, and
they seemed, by the expression of their faces, already
in thought upon the moorland road which was to lead
them to the frontier miles away, where very few of
us had ever been, and those few shook their heads with
a hint of dangers to be met, saying nothing but doubting
much, as the rest of us doubted, whether the brothers
ever were destined to achieve the purpose which they
all, though very indistinctly, had in view.

On the face of it the iconography is familiar. Young men
on bicycles were established emblems of aspiration, as in
Day Lewis's *The Magnetic Mountain*—'You who go out alone,
on tandem or on pillion'—or Edward Upward's sketch
'The Island', where 'these keen cyclists wearing the badge
of a worker's sports club on their leather jackets' are a
sign of the revolutionary future; Upward enlarged on the
idea towards the end of *Journey to the Border*, in which
the central figure, after his sudden conversion to revolutionary ideals, meets an inspiring young factory worker on
a bicycling holiday, who offers to put him in touch with
the workers' movement. Yet Warner's cyclists are not what
they seem; after another paragraph or so it is revealed
that they are riding *motor*-cycles. Unfortunately for Warner,
in the perspective of the fifties and sixties the motor-cyclist
has come to acquire a distinctly right-wing, even fascistic
significance. The frontier is a more central symbol, though
it does not have the same implication as in the days
of *New Country*, a few years before. It is still true that
a frontier implies a new country; but now the newness
suggests the sinister and the dangerous rather than the
revolutionary or the utopian. In Warner's novel the frontier
is not closely guarded; in fact, one can cross it without
realising that one has done so, but, once across, the traveller
is in a mysterious, cruel, arbitrary world that is an evident
simulacrum of a fascist regime. The three cyclists cross
the frontier and are not heard of again for years. Warner's
long, episodic narrative follows the fortunes of the most
active brother, George. *The Wild Goose Chase* has not worn

well, though an American critic, John McCormick, thinks
very highly of it.[12] There is little variation in stylistic
register, which leads to monotony, and so does the ultimately
deadening accumulation of random bizarre events. Some
of the descriptive writing is still fresh and vigorous, notably
the account of the revolutionary war, but the overall sense
is that Warner is not in full control of the different narrative
levels he wishes to employ. He moves from crude allegory
to the genuine symbolism of the wild geese and back again
disconcertingly, and the anti-totalitarian satire lacks coherence or plausibility. The book is heavily influenced by
Kafka, whose works had recently been translated into English
by Edwin and Willa Muir, and it shows the existing thirties
inclination to fable, as exemplified in the Mortmere stories
or Auden's 'Paid on Both Sides' and *The Orators*, being
reinforced by the example of the great Czech allegorist.
But Warner displays a reductive determination to read
Kafka in political rather than metaphysical terms.

Ruthven Todd's *Over the Mountain* (1939) has a similar
structure and import to *The Wild Goose Chase* and may
have been influenced by it; but it is shorter and, I think,
more entertaining. The narrator, known only as Michael,
is the son of an eccentric clergyman in a nameless village
at the foot of a high mountain, beyond which there is
rumoured to exist a strange unvisited land. Various expeditions have attempted to climb the mountain barrier but
without success. Then Michael tries, with a minimum of
preparation, and, although he experiences strange hallucinations and almost perishes on the climb, he succeeds in
crossing over into the 'new country' on the other side.
He finds a heightened and more disagreeable version of contemporary England, rather than the uncontrolled fantasy of
Warner's fictional world. Todd's novel, though, does have
things in common with Warner's, as in the prevalence
of a police force who are childish but cruel and trigger-
happy. (Todd's police also have a passion for eating sweets,
and in the end are revealed to be specially-trained imbecile
children.) There seems to be an element of Kafka in *Over
the Mountain*, but there are also strong suggestions of Mortmere, perhaps derived from the Auden–Isherwood plays.

(It is, I suppose, possible that Todd had read the Mortmere stories in manuscript, but not very likely, as he was not in touch with the Auden–Isherwood–Upward group.) One sees for instance a similar comic presentation of stock English types: the sanctimonious clergyman, Father Podmore; Colonel Roscoe, the former explorer and now director of the police; Mr Harold Boswell, an accentric headmaster; Sir Harry Bracesplit, a liberal newspaper-owner and sporting baronet. Indeed, the central theme of mountain climbing and much of the local detail is strongly reminiscent of *The Ascent of F6*. At the end the hero tries to return to his own country, and, indeed, thinks he has done so. But he then discovers that his own name is really Michael Podmore, so that his father and Father Podmore are the same man, and the other world, 'over the mountain', and his own are in fact indistinguishable. It is a rather thin conclusion to a spirited if derivative fable.

Edward Upward's mastery of a certain kind of English surrealistic fable, as evident in 'The Railway Accident', had antedated the English impact of Kafka by several years. His ideological progress is apparent in the few pieces of short fiction that he published in the thirties; 'The Colleagues' and 'Sunday' in *New Country*, and 'The Island' in *Left Review* in 1935. With his short novel *Journey to the Border* (1938), Upward continued to use the fabular vein that he had once devoted to Mortmere, but in a wholly didactic fashion. *Journey to the Border* has an emblematic title, which indicates the action of the narrative in figurative but unambiguous fashion. The young man who provides the central consciousness of the story is unhappy and unfulfilled in his job as private tutor in a repulsive bourgeois family. Reluctantly accompanying his employer to a race-meeting, he undergoes a series of hallucinations which convince him of the necessity of political revolution. Emerging from his delusions, he hears a voice in his head commenting on his experience, saying that he has been in a no-man's-land between sanity and insanity: 'Your condition could be best described, in clinical language, as "on the border".' But now, the voice continues, the tutor must learn to solve his problems, not in the mind alone, nor in the emotions, but in the real world of 'living practical action'. And this means joining the workers' movement. The tutor assents, at first reluctantly, then eagerly. The voice now uses the familiar image of crossing a frontier to a new country:

> You will have to move out of the region of thinking and feeling altogether, to cross over the frontier into effective action. For a short time you will be in an unfamiliar country. You will have taken your so-called 'plunge in the dark'; but it will not be in the dark for very long. Out of action your thinking and your feeling will be born again. A new thinking and a new feeling.

Upward still preserved the sentiments and the tone of *New Country* and the early thirties, just as he remained a member of the Communist Party long after his literary contemporaries had given up any inclination to Marxism.

In the same year as *Journey to the Border* Auden and Isherwood published the last and weakest of their collaborative verse plays, *On the Frontier*. The title may recall Upward's novella, but little else does. The frontier is real enough, dividing the two imaginary powers of Ostnia and Westland, which had first featured in *The Dog Beneath the Skin*; indeed, in some scenes the stage is divided by a symbolic frontier. But in a broader sense the 'frontier' in this play has no real significance. It is not like the metaphorical frontier dividing the bourgeois from the revolutionary consciousness, or the present from the future; or the border between France and Republican Spain, or the ultimate frontier between clashing ideologies provided by the front-line in Spain. The underlying attitude in *On the Frontier* is a 'plague on both your houses'. Westland is a modern fascist power, with a neurotic dictator; while Ostnia is an old-fashioned absolute monarchy (reminiscent, perhaps, of the Romania of King Carol). Both powers are aggressive and militaristic; they go to war, and civilisation collapses. Pity is directed to the victims on both sides. During the war, one of the Westland characters, Dr Thorvald, of whom it is said in

the stage directions, he 'would have been a liberal under
a democratic regime', reflects:

> You see, I was brought up to think that a man's greatest
> privilege was to fight for his country; and it's hard
> to change one's ideas. Perhaps we were all wrong. War
> seems so beastly when it actually happens! Perhaps
> 'country' and 'frontier' are old-fashioned words that don't
> mean anything now.   (III. i)

Samuel Hynes says of this passage:

> One is reminded of the *paysage moralisé* of Auden's earlier
> poems. In those poems, the frontier was always a place
> up ahead, beyond which was a New Country. But now,
> in 1938, he was *on* the frontier, and 'country' and 'frontier'
> were words that had no meaning. The words had symbo-
> lized a courageous and adventurous quest into the un-
> known; but in the war that was coming there would
> be no adventure, and courage would be useless, and
> the worst of the unknown would become familiar.[13]

On the Frontier is indeed a play without ideological clash
or commitment, and its implied positives are limited to
pacifism and humanitarianism. Politics has disappeared
to be replaced by the moralised psychologism that provided
Auden's frame of reference for the rest of his life. In
this respect *On the Frontier* is almost a post-thirties work;
one of those texts published in 1938–9 that were imaginati-
vely obsessed with the coming war, like MacNeice's *Autumn
Journal* and Orwell's *Coming Up for Air*.

IV

In 1938, too, a precocious schoolboy contributed a short
poem to *New Verse*. This was Keith Douglas's 'Dejection'.
It uses the typical imagery of 'country', and, in a semantic
variation on 'frontier' or 'border', the 'boundary'.

> Yesterday travellers in Autumn's country,
> Tonight the sprinkled moon and ravenous sky
> Say, we have reached the boundary. The autumn
>   clothes
> Are on; Death is the season and we the living
> Are hailed by the solitary to join their regiment,
> To leave the sea and the horses and march away
> Endlessly. The spheres speak with persuasive voices.

Douglas was only sixteen when he wrote this deft Audenesque exercise, as accomplished in its way as John Cornford's lines had been several years earlier.[14] Both poets died in war. September 1939 meant a new frontier or boundary; in due course Douglas put on the 'autumn clothes' of a khaki uniform, joined his regiment and marched away, to death in Normandy in 1944. Still in 1938, in the autumn of that year, Louis MacNeice wrote of the Munich crisis and the inevitability of war:

> The bloody frontier
>   Converges on our beds
> Like jungle beaters closing in on their destined
>   Trophy of pelts and heads.
> And at this hour of the day it is no good saying
>   'Take away this cup';
> Having helped to fill it ourselves it is only logic
>   That now we should drink it up.
>   (*Autumn Journal*, V)

The 'bloody frontier' was a new locution. Once the war started frontiers melted away, and the central literary symbol of a decade lost its point and purpose, though it persisted for a while. In 'Farewell Chorus', dated 'New Year 1940', David Gascoyne wrote:

> Nor may we return
> Except in unimpassioned recollections from beyond
> That ever-nearer frontier that our fate has drawn.

And Roy Fuller, stoically responding to the new situation

of beleagured wartime England, wrote in 'Summer 1940',

> The edges of the country are fraying with
> Too much use; the ports are visited by wrath
> In the shapes of the metal diver and the dart
> With screaming feathers and explosive heart.
>
> And the ships are guilty of a desire to return
> To land, to three mile pits and moulding urn.
> England no longer is shaped like a begging dog,
> Its shape is the shape of a state in the central bog,
>
> With frontiers which change at the yawn of a tired
>   ruler;
> At last the push of time has reached it; realer
> Today than for centuries, England is on the map
> As a place where something occurs, as a spring-board
>   or trap.

The map, another favourite Audenesque image, continued
to be usable. Maps, after all, are much in evidence in
wartime. But the frontiers went.

5 The Last Days of Futurism

There are some lines from Auden's 1930 *Poems* that soon became famous. At the end of the obscure but evocative sonnet that begins 'Sir, no man's enemy' we read,

> Harrow the house of the dead; look shining at
> New styles of architecture, a change of heart.

The contrast between new and old is typical of early Auden; a phrase that might have come from Old or Middle English poetry is juxtaposed with an image of modernity. Before long these lines became a kind of slogan and a matter for casual allusion, as when Lawrence Durrell writes in *The Black Book* (1938), 'New styles in the soul's architecture, new change of heart.' Nevertheless, in later years Auden came to regret these words, like much of his early poetry. He excluded 'Sir, no man's enemy' from his *Collected Shorter Poems* in 1966, and wrote in the foreword of that volume: 'I once expressed a desire for "New styles of architecture"; but I have never liked modern architecture. I prefer *old* styles, and one must be honest even about one's prejudices.' Despite this dismissal, the lines remain significant, and not just as an index of what Auden was interested in, or thought he was interested in, at the start of his career. Closely associated with modern architecture as an idea of newness were aeroplanes and airmen. In another well-known poem in the 1930 volume Auden wrote,

> Consider this and in our time
> As the hawk sees it or the helmeted airman . . . .

The lines are again highly characteristic. The hawk is a traditional symbol and the airman a modern one, but both are, in different ways, masters of the world they survey; the poem opens out into a brilliant example of Auden's panoramic manner. Elsewhere Auden used the airman as an image of modernity combined with poised, calm control, notably in *The Orators*. (And a similar iconography pervaded a famous film, written by H. G. Wells, *Things to Come*.) A few years later Auden wrote in one of the choruses in *The Dog Beneath the Skin*,

> Man is changed by his fate; but not fast enough.
> His concern today is for that which yesterday
> did not occur.
> In the hour of the Blue Bird and the Bristol
> Bomber, his thoughts are appropriate to
> the years of the Penny Farthing.

By now these particular images of technical advance and modernity, powerful enough in 1935, have themselves acquired an antiquarian flavour and may require explanation: the Blue Bird was Sir Malcolm Campbell's record-breaking racing car, and the Bristol Bomber was a prototype of the Blenheim, a widely-used aircraft of World War II. Other writers of the thirties were excited by aeroplanes and modern architecture and design, and other forms of technological innovation, and tried to identify them with a 'change of heart' or a revolutionary consciousness. Stephen Spender comes particularly to mind, with such poems as 'Pylons', 'The Express' and 'The Landscape Near an Aerodrome'. Indeed, the young poets of the thirties were journalistically dubbed the 'Pylon Poets'. Yet a doubt remains about whether such writing was as innovating as it seemed; to see it in perspective one needs to turn to the European context in the years immediately before the First World War.

The Futurist movement flourished in Italy from 1909 to about 1915. It may be surprising that in trying to trace the motifs of technical modernity in English writing one has to look back in time, and to another country.

Nevertheless, just as many of the features of twentieth-century technology—the motor-car, the aeroplane, the radio, the cinema—already existed in 1914, so too did most of the aesthetic modes and innovations that we continue to think of as avant-garde or revolutionary. It is difficult to exaggerate the importance of Futurism in this respect, since it sponsored such things as abstract painting, concrete poetry, *musique concrète* and mixed-media activities well over sixty years ago. At about that time, too, T. E. Hulme, in England, wrote an essay called 'Romanticism and Classicism', which called for a new anti-Romantic poetry that would be precise, cool, intelligent and cheerful, which is very much what the young English poets of the thirties came to write. The Futurists, led by the poet F. T. Marinetti, were very Italian, in that they liked noise, excitement and broad expansive gestures. Italy was an under-industrialised country, and at the same time full to the point of weariness with the great art of the past; so the Futurists preferred the unfamiliar beauty and excitement of machinery to the venerable contents of the galleries. In the first Futurist manifesto of 1909, Marinetti praised a racing car in these words: 'A racing car whose hood is adorned with great pipes, like serpents of explosive breath—a roaring car that seems to ride on grapeshot is more beautiful than the Victory of Samothrace.'[1] In this manifesto, published in the year in which Blériot flew the Channel, Marinetti praises 'the sleek flight of planes whose propellors chatter in the wind like banners and seem to cheer like an enthusiastic crowd'. From the beginning the Futurists were enthusiastic about flying and references to aeroplanes recur in their manifestos. In 1912 Marinetti opened his 'Technical Manifesto of Futurist Literature' with the arresting sentence,

> Sitting on the gas tank of an aeroplane, my stomach warmed by the pilot's head, I sensed the ridiculous inanity of the old syntax inherited from Homer.[2]

The titles of Futurist poems speak for themselves; indeed as early as 1909 one of the Futurist poets, Paolo Buzzi, published a collection called simply *Aeroplani*. Later instances include 'Flying Over the Heart of Italy' and 'The Futurist Airman Speaks to His Father, the Volcano' by Marinetti; 'To an Airman' by Libero Altomare; and 'Aeroplane Flight' by Enrico Cavacchiolo. The French poet Guillaume Apollinaire, who was closely associated with the Italian Futurists, refers in his long poem 'Zone' to aeroplane hangars as an ultimate symbol of modernity; in this poem he also describes Jesus Christ ascending into heaven as 'the first aeroplane'. All these references date from before the outbreak of the First World War. In this perspective Auden's helmeted airman looks like a latecomer rather than an innovator, and his lines from *The Dog Beneath the Skin*—'In the hour of the Blue Bird and the Bristol Bomber, his thoughts are appropriate to the years of the Penny Farthing'—might have been adapted from a Futurist poem or manifesto of twenty-five years earlier.

In '1929' (Poem XVI of the 1930 *Poems*) Auden wrote,

> Yet sometimes men look and say good
> At strict beauty of locomotive . . . .

The idea was shortly enlarged on by Spender in 'The Express', which reads almost like an expansion of sentiments from Marinetti's first manifesto: 'We will sing of . . . deep-chested locomotives whose wheels paw the tracks like the hooves of enormous steel horses bridled by tubing.' Spender's poem begins:

> After the first powerful, plain manifesto
> The black statement of pistons, without more fuss
> But gliding like a queen, she leaves the station.

There follows an evocation of mechanical speed and power, of a thoroughly Futurist kind:

> It is now she begins to sing—at first quite low
> Then loud, and at last with a jazzy madness—
> The song of her whistle screaming at curves,
> Of deafening tunnels, brakes, innumerable bolts.

Just as Marinetti had ebulliently preferred the racing car to the Greek sculpture, so at the end of the poem Spender prefers, or tries to prefer, the noise of the train to the traditional music of nature:

> Ah, like a comet through flame, she moves
>   entranced,
> Wrapt in her music no bird song, no, nor bough
> Breaking with honey buds, shall ever equal.

Spender may not have known much about Futurism when he wrote 'The Express', but we may still call it a Futurist poem, though written distinctly late in the day.[3]

One of the most interesting of the Futurists was the young architect Antonio Sant'Elia, who was killed in the First World War before he had been able to realise any of his ambitious projects. Sant'Elia is regarded by historians of modern architecture as an important forerunner of Le Corbusier and Walter Gropius, but for my present purposes I am most interested in a single phrase from his 'Manifesto of Futuristic Architecture', which has the characteristic vigour and iconoclasm of the other Futurist manifestos. (The Futurists were all very young men at the time.) Sant'Elia's manifesto was published in 1914, and in the course of it he writes, in capital letters for emphasis, 'ARCHITECTURE NOW MAKES A BREAK WITH TRADITION. IT MUST PERFORCE MAKE A FRESH START.'[4] These words closely anticipate Auden's 'New styles of architecture, a change of heart', though, again, I think it unlikely that Auden had heard of Sant'Elia or read his manifesto. But we can see that he was writing in a familiar-enough idiom. Sant'Elia did not live to see any of his plans turned into buildings. But one of the drawings that accompanied his manifesto illustrates the juxtaposition of new architecture and aeroplanes as images of modernity. As part of his proposed New City—*La Città Futurista*—Sant'Elia designed a structure that was intended to serve both as a station for trains and a landing-place for aeroplanes, though he may, in fact, have meant airships. Sant'Elia also left plans for electricity power stations. Electricity was by its very nature a powerful emblem of modernity, a point picked up by English poets in the early thirties. Auden wrote in 'Sir, no man's enemy', 'Send to us power and light', while in 'The Pylons' Spender wrote:

> But far above and far as sight endures
> Like whips of anger
> With lightning's danger
> There runs the quick perspective of the future.

After the First World War the new architecture that Sant'Elia had only dreamed of and projected was brought into reality. Walter Gropius founded the Bauhaus at Dessau in Germany, as a school of art and design for the machine age, which soon became internationally famous. In 1926 Gropius's teacher Peter Behrens designed an uncompromisingly modern house at Northampton for Mr Bassett-Lowke, a manufacturer of model railways. The house was called, suitably, 'New Ways', though the furniture was designed by Charles Rennie Mackintosh, thereby preserving a relationship with the *art nouveau* manner of pre-war days. Indeed, the stark angular manner associated with the Bauhaus spread to the ever-growing English suburbs, though it never rivalled the mock-Tudor idiom. Alan A. Jackson, in his book on the development of London suburbia, *Semi-Detached London*, remarks that in the twenties 'Gropius was building small houses at Dessau and elsewhere and English architects were providing designs in the new style for wealthy clients. With its flat roof, smooth white walls and large steel-framed windows, "Modern" fitted well with the contemporary sun-cult.'[5] In his manifesto of Futurist architecture, Sant'Elia had emphasised the importance of new building materials, notably concrete, steel, and glass. The same point was later made by Gropius in his influential book *The New Architecture and the Bauhaus*, of which the first English edition appeared in 1935. There Gropius writes, 'New synthetic substances—steel, concrete, glass—are actively superseding the traditional raw materials of construction.' Steel, concrete, glass were essential elements in the new architecture. Recently Rayner Banham has made the interesting sugges-

tion that in the field of design Futurism came to a climax
in the late thirties:

> So came the streamlined ships, the tear-drop cars, those
> classic trains like the Burlington Zephyr—and finally a
> whole streamlined future expounded in a series of exhibi-
> tions culminating in a *locus classicus* of Futurism if ever
> there was one, the New York World's Fair of 1939
> with its 'Highways and Horizons', 'Futurama', 'Democra-
> city', 'Road of the Future', its 'Rocketport'.[6]

One of the more bizarre characters in Evelyn Waugh's
first novel, *Decline and Fall* (1928), is the young German
architect Otto Friedrich Silenus, who is commissioned by
Margot Beste-Chetwynde to remake entirely her beautiful
and unspoilt Tudor mansion, King's Thursday, into 'Something clean and spare'. He first attracted her attention with
'the rejected design for a chewing-gum factory which had
been reproduced in a progressive Hungarian quarterly';
this was followed by the decor for an avant-garde film.
That is about all Silenus has to show for himself. Nevertheless, he makes a thorough job of King's Thursday, transform-
ing it into something very modern indeed, 'Roofs and
domes of glass and aluminium'. Silenus has strong opinions
on the subject of architecture, and believes as far as possible
in the elimination of the human element from the consider-
ation of form. He claims that 'The only perfect building
must be the factory, because that is built to house machines
not men. I do not think it is possible for domestic architecture
to be beautiful, but I am doing my best.' His reputation
soon grows: ' "I saw some of Otto Silenus's work at Munich,"
said Potts. "I think that he's a man worth watching. He
was in Moscow at one time and in the Bauhaus at Dessau." '
This passing comment may be the first reference to the
Bauhaus in English literature. Some of Silenus's ideas have
affinities with both the Futurists and the Bauhaus. The
fascination with factories was one instance; Silenus's unreal-
ised design for a chewing-gum factory was paralleled in
reality by Gropius's first major project, a boot-last factory,
built in Germany as early as 1911; a photograph of this

building appears as the first illustration in *The New Architecture and the Bauhaus*. It is certainly true that modern idioms were more quickly accepted in industrial design than in domestic or civic architecture.

Some English writers took a less sardonic view of the new styles of architecture than Evelyn Waugh. At the end of 'Pylons' Spender wrote,

> This dwarfs our emerald country by its trek
> So tall with prophecy:
> Dreaming of cities
> Where often clouds shall lean their swan-white neck.

I find this a particularly interesting image, since Spender concludes his praise of electricity and the new technology with a romantic, even lyrical, suggestion of the city of tomorrow outsoaring the clouds—perhaps even faintly personified, in a suggestion of Leda embraced by Jupiter in the form of a swan. The new architecture here seems to be assuming the poetic and transcendent quality of the celestial city or New Jerusalem of the Apocalypse. Others, though, remained ambivalent, like George Orwell in his poem of 1934 entitled 'On a Ruined Farm near the His Master's Voice Gramophone Factory'.[7] This presents an explicit and unresolved double vision. The new buildings of the gramophone factory are presented as a form of celestial city:

> The factory-towers, white and clear
> Like distant, glittering cities seen
> From a ship's rail . . . .

The towers contrast with the ruined farm and the smoke-soured fields. They stand for the future, yet the poet cannot accept their promise:

> But there, where steel and concrete soar
> In dizzy, geometric towers—

> There, where the tapering cranes sweep round,
> And great wheels turn, and trains roar by
> Like strong, low-headed brutes of steel—
> There is my world, my home; yet why
>
> So alien still? I can neither
> Dwell in that world, nor turn again
> To scythe and spade, but only loiter
> Among the trees the smoke has slain.

Orwell feels nothing of the Futurists' enthusiasm for the new technology and the civilisation it brings with it; he develops his uncertainty in what sounds like a conscious echo of Matthew Arnold's complaint about being 'Poised between two worlds, one dead, the other powerless to be born'. And there is a remarkably similar expression of feeling in Bernard Spencer's poem 'Suburb Factories', first published in *New Verse* in 1936. It concludes with these stanzas:

> From the diamonded parks I would wish to delight
> At shapes that attack and are new:
> But it's hard,
> Knowing only for certain; power is here surrendered
> And it changes to the hands of the few.
>
> Changes though; change is the air; roofscape
> Touches some nerve, and the lost
> Sinking scream
> Of electric trains touches it, and white masonry
> Springs up like a fire, but strikes like frost.

(The penultimate stanza was dropped when this poem was collected in Spencer's *Aegean Islands* in 1946.) This indecision persisted, however much cultural propagandists approved of the new styles. Some English architects did indeed welcome them, in the spirit of Sant'Elia and Le Corbusier and the Bauhaus, but men of letters did not, on the whole. The new structures of glass and concrete and steel were regarded as impressive, interesting or curious, but something external to English culture—unless, as was increasingly the case, this detached spirit deepened into positive hostility.

Graham Greene, whose early novels are full of meticulous observation of contemporary cultural processes, provides some valuable examples. In *England Made Me*, the crooked Swedish millionaire Krogh lives and works in a gleaming ultra-modern building in Stockholm, which is described as five floors of steel and glass, circular in shape with a courtyard and an illuminated fountain in the centre. Krogh is not at ease in the building, indeed scarcely understands why he has built it:

> On this building he had employed men whom he had been told were the best architects, sculptors, interior decorators in Sweden. He looked from the curved tuiya wood desk to the glass walls, from the clock without numerals to the statuette between the windows of a pregnant woman. He understood nothing. These things gave him no pleasure.   (Part II, ch. 1)

We share Krogh's vision of his elegant new building. And there is a similar reference in Greene's next novel, *A Gun for Sale*, published in 1936. The villain of that novel is another tycoon, a melodramatic, ancient figure, known simply as Sir Marcus. He is an armament manufacturer, a prominent type in the demonology of the thirties, and he is trying to start a European war for the profit of the arms trade. He is the head of an industrial organisation called Midland Steel, and has a very modern office in a Midland city, Nottwich. It is described as a 'great functional building of black glass and steel'. One could imagine it getting favourable mention in an architectural journal of the time, but in Greene's scheme it is a setting for monstrous crime and conspiracy.

The new styles of architecture evoked two principal responses: one, that they were alien, in a literal way, and two, that they made buildings or interiors seem to have different purposes or appearances from their true ones, thereby defeating the proposed ends of functionalism as an architectural creed. Consider, for instance, Christopher

Isherwood's Berlin diary of 1930, in *Goodbye to Berlin*. He
describes the house of the wealthy Bernstein family, which
is in the Grünewald, outside Berlin, and is 'built entirely
of glass'. He says of the interior,

> The hall of the Bernsteins' house has metal-studded doors
> and a steamer clock fastened to the wall with bolt-heads.
> There are modernist lamps designed to look like pressure
> gauges, thermometers, and switchboard dials.

Thus far, an interior that might have pleased the mechanical-
ly-minded futurists: 'the Futurist house must be like a
gigantic machine', wrote Sant'Elia in 1914, anticipating
Le Corbusier's idea of a house as a machine for living
in. To us, though, the Bernsteins' house, like Krogh's Swedish
palace, possesses the period charm of *art déco*. And in any
case, as Isherwood goes on to describe, in his flat ironic
way, the Bernsteins have done their best to muffle the
effect:

> But the furniture doesn't match the house and its fittings.
> The place is like a power station which the engineers
> have tried to make comfortable with chairs and tables
> from an old-fashioned, highly respectable boarding-house.
> On the austere metal walls hang highly varnished nine-
> teenth-century landscapes in massive gold frames. Herr
> Bernstein probably ordered the villa from a popular *avant-
> garde* architect in a moment of recklessness; was horrified
> at the result and tried to cover it up as much as possible
> with the family belongings.

The Berlin area at the time before Hitler when the Bauhaus
influence was at its height is also the setting for a hotel
described in Anthony Powell's novel *Agents and Patients*
(1936):

> The Sans Souci Palast was on a corner where four roads
> met. It stood back, half hidden by fir trees, a white
> building designed on modern principles with a wide
> enclosed veranda in front of it, the top of which made

a balcony for the rooms on the first floor. On the gravel space in front of the entrance were some green tables and chairs, rusty and piled on one another. There was no sign of life, and at first sight the place seemed to be an isolation hospital or a hydro, rather than a hotel. (Ch. 4)

It appeared to be a characteristic of modern buildings to look like something other than they were. In *Brighton Rock* Graham Greene refers to a crematorium in 'a bright new flowery suburb' which has 'two brick towers like those of a Scandinavian town hall'; and in his last pre-war novel, *The Confidential Agent* (1939), there is a curious seaside hotel: 'it was more like a village than a hotel as they came down towards it—or nearer comparison still, an air-port: circle after circle of chromium bungalows round a central illuminated tower—fields and more bungalows.' At close quarters it seems that the hotel is trying, in fact, to imitate an ocean liner, and the rooms are made to look exactly like cabins. As Greene later acknowledged, he had hit on an early version of a largely post-war pheno-menon, the holiday camp. But the casual reference to the airport is also significant, and another indication of Greene's remarkable prescience, for in recent years the airport seems to have become the supreme instance of the international modern style; though Apollinaire had seen the airport hangar as the apotheosis of modernity as long ago as 1913. (At the University of Warwick, where there is an abundance of glass and steel and concrete, one of the large assembly rooms is known as a matter of course as the 'airport lounge'.)

I now turn to the aeroplane itself, a pure symbol of modernity for the Futurist imagination, and one intimately associated with the new architecture. I have already referred to Spender's 'The Express' and 'The Pylons'; here are the opening lines of 'The Landscape Near an Aerodrome':

More beautiful and soft than any moth
With burring furred antennae feeling its huge path
Through dusk, the air-liner with shut-off engines

>   Glides over suburbs and sleeves set trailing tall
>   To point the wind.

It was part of the Futurist creed to insist on the superiority
of mechanical beauty to natural. So, in 'The Express',
Spender writes that the noise of the train is more beautiful
than birdsong; and in this poem the aeroplane is more
beautiful than any moth. Some of the contributors in *New
Country* tried to use the aeroplane as a symbol of political
revolution—as did the young Communist poet Richard
Goodman in 'The Squadrons':

>   Throbbing with strength with their desire to soar
>   through dawn, that barrage, bravely into day,
>   the squadrons wheel, immense, towards the sun
>   and roar
>   their voice like fire which tells of massive joy.[8]

Day Lewis, in Part XVI of *The Magnetic Mountain*, fulsomely
addressed Auden as 'Wystan, lone flyer, birdman, my bully
boy!', urging,

>   Gain altitude, Auden, then let the base beware!
>   Migrate, chaste my kestrel, you need a change of
>   air!

Auden had already made the Airman a central figure
of *The Orators*. But, as he later acknowledged, the ideological
implications of this figure were not necessarily of the Left.
In fact, the airman, the lone flyer, the aeroplane, tended
to be right-wing rather than left-wing symbols. They recur
in the early poetry of the Italian Futurists, and, as we
know, Futurism provided imaginative and ideological im-
petus to Fascism in Italy, and Marinetti became a life-long
Fascist. Indeed, one of the most effective iconic uses of
a solitary aeroplane is in the opening shot of Leni Reifens-
thal's brilliant and disturbing film *Triumph of the Will*,
showing Hitler flying in to open the 1934 Nuremberg Rally
of the Nazi Party. In the Soviet Union, the Russian wing
of the Futurist movement under Mayakovsky wanted to

give aesthetic expression to Communism in the twenties, but was shortly suppressed by Stalin.

In England the aeroplane was soon regarded by writers in much the same sceptical way as modern architecture. Once more, Graham Greene is a valuable witness. In *England Made Me* he shows himself keenly interested in aeroplanes. At one point a minor character in the story, Fred Hall, flies from Holland to Sweden on a regular flight of Royal Dutch Airlines; Greene devotes several pages to describing the flight, and the episode is given fuller treatment than is strictly necessary for the unfolding of the plot. Nevertheless, it is a fine piece of descriptive writing, providing a vivid sense of what air travel was like in the early thirties. Towards the end of the flight Greene sets out a series of sharp images, summing up the airports of Europe as the widely-travelled Fred Hall had known them. Supposedly we are sharing Fred Hall's thoughts, but, as often in Greene, the world-weary, omniscient author has taken over. We are given one of those lists full of adjectives and definite articles that are common in both the prose of Greene and the poetry of Auden and which typify the style of the period:

He knew the airports of Europe as well as he had once known the stations on the Brighton line—shabby Le Bourget; the great scarlet rectangle of the Tempelhof as one came in from London in the dark, the headlamp lighting up the asphalt way; the white sand blowing up round the shed at Tallin; Riga, where the Berlin to Leningrad plane came down and bright pink mineral waters were sold in a tin-roofed shed; the huge aerodrome at Moscow with machines parked half a dozen deep, the pilots taxi-ing casually here and there, trying to find room, bouncing back and forth, beckoned by one official with his cap askew. (Part V, ch. 3)

These images preserve a distinct historical moment, when the primitive airports of Europe still had a certain individuality. Within a few years airport design would become a ubiquitous international idiom, with no room for separate national identity. It seems like an objective piece of reporting, but there is a pervasive romanticism about this passage, an updated version of the nineteenth-century feeling about railway terminuses and the *poésie des départs*. But the romanticism is called up by the association of the places, not by their character as social and technological innovation. At the end of *England Made Me*, which is a story of crime and shady financial dealing in the highest places, of almost Jacobean intensity, a flight of aeroplanes appears in the air over Stockholm. As first presented they seem to have the aloof, dynamic beauty that the Futurists admired:

> up in the air behind him, wheeling over the lake, zooming down towards the City Hall, rising and falling like a flight of swallows, the sun catching their aluminium wings as they turned, came the aeroplanes, a dozen at least, making the air noisy with their engines . . . .   (Part VII)

But what are these aeroplanes doing? It soon becomes clear that their flight is no disinterested display of power and beauty. Their purpose is strictly commercial; they are there to make an advertisement for the criminal financier Krogh, writing his name in smoke in the sky above Stockholm: 'The aeroplanes drove back above the lake, leaving a plumy trail: "Krogh's. Krogh's," over Stockholm, a thin trellis-work of smoke; the "K" fading as the "S" was drawn'. In the immediate context of Greene's novel we are reminded that Krogh is still triumphant in the end, secure in his uncomfortable steel-and-glass palace, using the achievements of technology to write his name in the sky. Yet there is a larger irony. The aeroplane could still be seen as an impersonal symbol of power and speed and beauty. But it had practical uses, too, and not all of them were benign or appealing.

Aeroplanes could write advertisements in the sky; they could also drop bombs, and it was this latter use that came to dominate the literary imagination as the thirties passed and the international situation worsened. In *The Dog Beneath the Skin* Auden could still refer to 'the Blue Bird and the Bristol Bomber' as symbols of challenging modernity. But already the bomber had ceased to be a symbol and was becoming a frightful reality. Indeed, the historian Correlli Barnett has observed in his book *The Collapse of British Power* that in the early thirties 'the British were obsessed by fear of the bomber'[9] and suggests that British foreign policy tended to reflect this loss of nerve. A central episode in Greene's *A Gun for Sale* takes place during a mock air-raid on the city of 'Nottwich', the background to the novel being an international crisis brought about by Sir Marcus's machinations. Aeroplanes fly high over Sir Marcus's black glass and steel building, in a significant juxtaposition. In George Orwell's *Keep the Aspidistra Flying*, published in the same year as *A Gun for Sale*, 1936, the depressed hero, Gordon Comstock, regards the prospect of bombs dropping on London with apocalyptic relish: 'And the reverberations of future wars. Enemy aeroplanes flying over London; the deep threatening hum of the propellors, the shattering thunder of the bombs.' Such reflections recur at regular intervals throughout this novel. A year later this apocalyptic mood was savagely expressed in John Betjeman's famous poem 'Slough', which looks for a violent encounter of the bomb and the bright, hygenic, technological world:

> Come, friendly bombs, and fall on Slough!
> It isn't fit for humans now,
> There isn't grass to graze a cow.
>   Swarm over, Death!

> Come, bombs, and blow to smithereens
> Those air-conditioned, bright canteens,
> Tinned fruit, tinned meat, tinned milk, tinned beans,
>   Tinned minds, tinned breath.

Images of bombing were increasingly common in the poetry of the later thirties, particularly after aerial bombing became widespread during the Spanish Civial War. As, for instance, in Auden's 'Danse Macabre':

> It's farewell to the drawing-room's mannerly cry,

> The professor's logical whereto and why,
> The frock-coated diplomat's polished aplomb,
> Now matters are settled with gas and with bomb

or C. Day Lewis's 'Bombers':

> Black as vermin, crawling in echelon
> Beneath the cloud-floor, the bombers come:
> The heavy angels, carrying harm in
> Their wombs that ache to be rid of death.

Other poems, by Herbert Read and George Barker, express horrified responses to reports of the bombing of civilians in Spain. Even in books of the period that are not specifically concerned with the threat of war and bombing, such possibilities occur as metaphor. Thus, in Graham Greene's *Brighton Rock* there are some extravagant but significant images; where, as so often, the author takes over from the limited consciousness of his characters. Here, for instance, is Rose looking at Ida: 'She watched the woman closely: she would never forget that plump, good-natured, ageing face: it stared out at her like an idiot's from the ruins of a bombed house.' And a page or so later Ida looks back at Rose: 'The bony and determined face stared back at her: all the fight there was in the world lay there—warships cleared for action and bombing fleets took flight between the set eyes and the stubborn mouth.' The mood of Betjeman's 'Slough' is amplified in the last of Orwell's pre-war novels, *Coming Up for Air.* Orwell's fiction, like Greene's, combined strong, even obsessive, personal preoccupations with direct social observation. In this novel, Orwell's middle-aged, middle-class hero, George Bowling, takes a few days' holiday from his nagging wife and the dull suburb where he lives. He goes to the village of Lower Binfield, where he had enjoyed the pleasures of rural life as a boy, and where he hopes to recapture the spirit of his youth. But Lower Binfield, when he reaches it, has been quite spoilt; built over, modernised, and turned into yet one more expanse of uniform semi-suburbia:

And the newness of everything! The raw, mean look! Do you know the look of these new towns that have suddenly swelled up like balloons in the last few years, Hayes, Slough, Dagenham, and so forth? The kind of chilliness, the bright red brick everywhere, the temporary-looking shop-windows full of cut-price chocolates and radio parts. It was just like that. (Part IV, ch. 1)

George Bowling is very much a vehicle for Orwell's vision of English life, and his responses suggest that the troubled ambivalence expressed in Orwell's poem of 1934, 'On a Ruined Farm near the His Master's Voice Gramophone Factory' has now been resolved into outright rejection of the new architecture of the factory and the way of life associated with it. As Bowling looks down on the town, the factory and the bomber are brought into the same focus:

Towards the eastern end of the town there were two enormous factories of glass and concrete. That accounts for the growth of the town, I thought, as I began to take it in. . . . As I looked a fleet of black bombing planes came over the hill and zoomed across the town.

In Lower Binfield there is much talk of bombs. Indeed, George discovers that they are manufactured there. A barmaid says of the inhabitants, 'Well, they mostly work at the factories. There's the gramophone works, and there's Truefitt Stockings. But of course they're making bombs nowadays.' At the end of the novel a bomb is actually dropped on Lower Binfield, accidently discharged from an R.A.F. plane on a practice raid; it destroys a house and kills three people. *Coming Up for Air*, published just before the outbreak of war in 1939, is both a farewell to the thirties and an anticipation of the war to come. It has something of the finality of Louis MacNeice's *Autumn Journal*, published at the same time, or Auden's poem '1st September 1939', or Patrick Hamilton's slightly later novel, *Hangover Square*.

At the beginning of the decade, I believe, poets such

as Auden and Spender and Day Lewis wanted to incorporate the modern world into their poems, and particularly its technology and the small-scale, day-to-day manifestations of mass society, or urban and suburban life. Eliot had done as much, of course, but in his own highly idiosyncratic way, which turned his observations of the contemporary scene into haunting but somewhat impalpable images, in the symbolist manner. There is a good summary of the process in Karl Shapiro's *Essay on Rime*. He writes of Auden and his disciples,

> For the first time the radio
> The car, the sofa and the new highway
> Came into focus in a poem as things,
> Not symbols of the things. The scenery changed
> To absolute present and the curtain rose
> On the actual place, not Crane's demonic city
> Nor Eliot's weird unreal metropolis,
> But that pedestrian London with which prose
> Alone had previously dealt.[10]

That is nicely put, and in the mid-forties it could still seem a true placing of the achievement of the Auden generation. Now, however, Shapiro's summary looks a good deal too simple. Literature does not easily assimilate things-in-themselves, or the 'absolute present', without mediating codes and models. At the very beginning of their careers, Auden and Spender, though seemingly looking forward, were in fact reaching back to the great matrix of ideas and possibilities that formed European modernism in the years just before the First World War. It provided modes and images whereby the 'absolute present' could be presented and even celebrated. A developing pattern can be found in the thirties where these forms of modernity, the 'new styles of architecture'—and *a fortiori* 'the change of heart'— and the aeroplane, came to seem less and less symbolically convincing to the literary imagination. This is true of both poets and novelists, in so far as the latter are concerned not only with story-telling and character, but also with metaphor and imagery and all the many subtexts that comprise a work of fiction. In reproducing the data of contemporary society, poets and novelists used similar codes and patterns of mediation.

If the appeal of modernity faded, history is perhaps most to blame. It is hard to feel idealistic about aeroplanes if they are dropping bombs on you, or to romanticise fine new buildings of steel and glass and concrete if they are used for criminal conspiracies, or even the manufacture of bombs. Yet the new styles of architecture did persist in England in the thirties and were still much admired by other kinds of artist. It was only the writers who became sceptical. What was exciting in Italy between 1910 and 1914 seemed no longer so in England in 1936, and it is perhaps an implication of my argument that in literary terms Futurism had its final moment in England in the early thirties. In other non-literary and specifically material and military ways it transformed itself in its native land to Fascism and the posturings of Mussolini, who loved aeroplanes and who threatened to darken the sky with his bombers. Yet we may be faced with something deeper than simple historical change. It may be true, and I think it can be shown, that in England, at least, the literary imagination is conservative, that literature is not capable of the same degree of radical renovation as the other arts. Stephen Spender has argued along these lines in *The Struggle of the Modern*. Indeed, the great achievements of the modern movement in literature were to some extent rediscoveries. Steel and glass and concrete were wholly new elements, and have totally transformed architecture all over the world; even if to nobody's great satisfaction. Yet they seemed, in the end, unassimilable into literature in any permanent fashion. Literature, like the human organism, may have its rejection processes. This, certainly, is the feeling expressed in a poem by the late David Jones, who was both a painter and a writer; very much a literary modernist, a follower of Eliot and Joyce, whilst at the same time a craftsman and a Catholic traditionalist. This poem was begun in the thirties, though not finished until much later, for it is dated '1938–1966'. Like much of Jones's writing it combines verse and prose. His vision of art was sacramental and archetypal; he records trying to find the possibilities of art and symbol, and the traces of divinity, in the new forms and materials, but failing.

> I have journeyed among the dead forms
> causation projects from pillar to pylon . . . .

> I have been on my guard
>   not to condemn the unfamiliar.
> For it is easy to miss Him
>   at the turn of a civilization

I have watched the wheels go round in case I might see the living creatures like the appearance of lamps, in case I might see the Living God projected from the Machine. I have said to the perfected steel, be my sister and for the glassy towers I thought I felt some beginnings of His creature, but *A, a, a, Domine Deus*, my hands found the glazed work unrefined and the terrible crystal a stage-paste. . . . *Eia, Domine Deus.*[11]

The ultimate irony is that Auden, who deleted the reference to 'new styles of architecture' from his *Collected Shorter Poems*, and who immensely admired David Jones, would probably have agreed with these sentiments.

6 Supplying the Lyrics

'Strange how potent cheap music is,' remarked Amanda to Elyot at a tender moment in Noël Coward's *Private Lives*. In this century some of the most serious writers have responded to the potency of music that, if not necessarily cheap, is certainly popular—ragtime and jazz and blues— and have woven it into their work. When T. S. Eliot was composing *The Waste Land* his mind echoed with ragtime tunes that he had heard in the music-halls of Boston before 1914, and he quoted or alluded to several of them in the early drafts of the poem. Most of these references did not survive Ezra Pound's editorial revisions, since Pound, unlike Eliot, had no taste for popular entertainment; but in the final version 'that Shakespeherian rag' remains, recalling a hit song of 1912. In *Sweeney Agonistes*, which Arnold Bennett described as a 'jazz play', Eliot provided his own ragtime lyrics. At about the same time, in 1925, Scott Fitzgerald published *The Great Gatsby*, a novel much admired by Eliot, which is shot through with allusions to popular songs: 'There was music from my neighbour's house throughout the summer nights.' Fitzgerald brings in some celebrated songs of the jazz age: 'The Sheik of Araby', 'Ain't We Got Fun', 'Three O'Clock in the Morning', culminating in a vivid sentence, finely poised between sentimentality and true romantic feeling: 'All night the saxophones wailed the hopeless comment of the "Beale Street Blues" while a hundred pairs of golden and silver slippers shuffled the shining dust.' (Two years before, in *Leave it to Psmith*, P. G. Wodehouse had made a cooler reference to 'that

curious composition known as the "Beale Street Blues" '.)
As a very young man another novelist, Malcolm Lowry,
with a friend of his, actually wrote and published two
fox-trots, 'I've Said Goodbye to Shanghai' and 'Three Little
Dog-Gone Mice'.[1] This circumstance forms one of the many
autobiographical motifs that Lowry later worked into *Under
the Volcano*.

In the thirties, the popular song, already widely available
on gramophone records, came into even fuller social consciousness with the arrival of the talkies, and was brought
into almost every home by radio. Auden and MacNeice
were both very aware of the idiom and used it freely
in their poetry. Auden, always a protean imitator of current
forms, wrote many blues and torch songs, some of the
best of which are grouped together as 'Twelve Songs' in
Part II of the *Collected Shorter Poems*. Four of them were
originally published in *Another Time* under the heading
'Four Cabaret Songs for Miss Hedli Anderson'. They include
the plangent 'Funeral Blues', which had appeared in an
earlier version in *The Ascent of F6*:

> Stop all the clocks, cut off the telephone,
> Prevent the dogs from barking with a juicy bone,
> Silence the pianos and with muffled drum
> Bring out the coffin, let the mourners come.

Another of these Cabaret Songs is 'O Tell Me the Truth
About Love', a spirited and witty version of a catalogue
song in the Cole Porter manner. (Graham Greene, we
recall, had referred in 1936 to the 'Audenesque charm'
of 'You're the Top':)

> Does it howl like a hungry Alsatian
>   Or boom like a military band,
> Could one give a first-class imitation
>   On a saw or a Steinway Grand,
> Is its singing at parties a riot,
>   Does it only like Classical stuff,
> Will it stop when one wants to be quiet?
>   O tell me the truth about love.

The catalogue song was evidently congenial to Auden, since it was close in form and spirit to his own more serious poetry, and there are other examples in his plays, particularly *The Dog Beneath the Skin*:

> If Chanel gowns have a train this year,
>   If Morris cars fit a self-changing gear,
> If Lord Peter Wimsey
>   Misses an obvious clue,
> If Wallace Beery
> Should act a fairy
>   And Chaplin the Wandering Jew;
> The reason is
> Just simply this:
>   They're in the racket, too!

Auden's songs are virtuoso exercises, tending to the witty and cynical rather than the sentimental or nostalgic. But there is a pleasant pastiche of a sentimental song in his early play, *The Dance of Death*, which has rather more of a *cantabile* quality than his later songs, and suggests the way in which the best thirties lyrics could sometimes evoke genuine poignancy through a flippant manner:

> You were a great Cunarder, I
> Was only a fishing smack
> Once you passed across my bows
> And of course you did not look back
> It was only a single moment yet
> I watch the sea and sigh
> Because my heart can never forget
> The day you passed me by.

In MacNeice's poetry the use of popular song is less of a deliberate pastiche or performance than it is in Auden, and closer to the centre of MacNeice's poetic art. Like Auden, he could deftly pick up a contemporary idiom, as in the opening of 'Hymn of the Collectors' in his play *Out of the Picture*. This combines a *cantabile* movement with a list of smart, evocative items, rather in the manner of

'These Foolish Things':

> Spring comes with drums and jonquils
> And smells of French fern soap
> And telephones keep ringing
> Insistent bells of hope . . . .

MacNeice's poetic persona, balancing irony and sentimentality, cynicism and nostalgia, had affinities with the characteristic spirit of songs by Noël Coward or Ira Gershwin or Cole Porter. At the same time, many of his shorter poems in regular stanzas are in a central tradition of English lyrical or ballad poetry, reaching back beyond literary models to carols and folk-songs. At their best, they bring together the traditional and the modern. Thus, one of MacNeice's finest lyrics, 'The Sunlight on the Garden', unites personal feelings and a sense of public crisis in verse of great verbal dexterity, reminiscent of Cole Porter or Ira Gershwin:

> And not expecting pardon,
> Hardened in heart anew,
> But glad to have sat under
> Thunder and rain with you,
> And grateful too
> For sunlight on the garden.

In *Autumn Journal*, too, MacNeice used the idiom of the popular song in a genuinely creative way to express his grief for a lost love:

And the train's rhythm becomes the *ad nauseam* repetition
Of every tired aubade and maudlin madrigal,
The faded airs of sexual attraction
   Wandering like dead leaves along a warehouse wall:
'I loved my love with a platform ticket,
   A jazz song,
A handbag, a pair of stockings of Paris Sand—
   I loved her long.'

It is not surprising that poets should write songs. What is less expected is that a distinguished novelist of the thirties generation should also imitate popular songs and systematically introduce them into his novels. I am referring to Graham Greene. His first book was a collection of undergraduate verse, and he has published occasional poems throughout his career. But the songs in his pre-war novels make him almost an honorary thirties poet. Greene published nine novels between 1929 and 1939. The first of them, *The Man Within*, is a historical novel. The next two, *The Name of Action* and *Rumour at Nightfall*, have never been reprinted, as Greene regarded them as inferior work and effectively suppressed them. Of the remaining books, *Stamboul Train*, *A Gun for Sale* and *The Confidential Agent* were published as 'entertainments', and *It's a Battlefield*, *England Made Me* and *Brighton Rock* were 'novels'. But the distinction was always somewhat factitious, and Greene has dropped it in the Collected Edition of his works. So I shall refer to all these books as 'novels'.

One of the characters in *Stamboul Train* is an early version of a type who recurs throughout Greene's fiction: Coral Musker, a frail, vulnerable girl with unexpected reserves of toughness. She is a chorus-girl, travelling across Europe to join a song-and-dance act in Istanbul. During a delay on the journey she is asked to sing something to pass the time. She provides a bitter-sweet, would-be sophisticated piece, very much of the period:

> I was sitting in a car
>   With Michael;
> I looked at a star
>   With John;
> I had a glass of bitter
>   With Peter
>   In a bar;
> But the pips went wrong; they never go right,
>   This year, next year
> (You may have counted wrong, count again, dear),
>   Some day, never.
> I'll be a good girl for ever and ever.

This song is no more than decorative; or at best a metonymic expression of the kind of girl Coral is. But at the end of the book Greene uses a song in a more functional way, deriving from one of the great literary innovations of the nineteenth century. In the agricultural-show episode of *Madame Bovary* Flaubert had shown how two clashing codes of discourse could be set against each other: expressions of love and passion counterpointed with banalities about prize-winning cattle and produce. It has since become a central narrative device in novels and films. The cinema, in particular, can exploit the ironic possibilities of dissonance between what is being presented in images and the accompanying sounds, whether in words or music. And the ubiquitous radio set makes such an effect instantly available, in the most realistic context.[2] So, at the end of *Stamboul Train*, Myatt and Janet Pardoe are watching a cabaret in Istanbul, at the same time engaged on serious conversation. Their talk is punctuated by the English chorus girls cheerfully singing a wistfully erotic lyric:

> If you want to express
> That feeling you've got,
> When you're sometimes cold, sometimes hot.
>
> If you want to express
> That kind of gloom
> You feel alone in a double room . . . .

There is a more melodramatic—and cinematic—use of the device in *England Made Me*. The setting is a Swedish hotel: in the entrance hall a man is brutally beaten up, while in the restaurant the orchestra plays a plaintive torch-song:

> I'm waiting, dear,
> Leave off hating, dear,
> Let's talk of mating, dear,
> I'm lonely.
>
> You can't ration, dear,
> The kind of passion, dear,
> Though it's not the fashion, dear . . . .

Anne Crowder, the heroine of Greene's next novel, *A Gun for Sale*, is, like Carol Musker, a chorus-girl, whose personality combines resourcefulness and touching innocence. In the first chapter, before the action begins, Anne plays a gramophone record she has just bought. 'She put on the new record, hugging to her heart the silly senseless words, the slow sleepy tune':

> It's only Kew
> To you,
> But to me
> It's Paradise.
> They are just blue
> Petunias to you,
> But to me
> They are your eyes.
> They say that's a snowflower
> A man brought from Greenland,
> I say it's the lightness, the coolness, the whiteness
> Of your hand.

The song is recalled throughout the novel, as Anne remembers snatches of it at moments of violence or danger. It is, I think, one of Greene's most accomplished compositions in this genre, and good enough to be the real commercial article; the prosody nicely suggests 'the slow sleepy tune'. The lines are significant in another way, too. In 1936 Greene was not famous enough for critics to have started talking about 'Greeneland', but the phrase 'A man brought from Greenland' anticipates that inescapable critical cliché. (An early example, perhaps, of the strange prescience that later enabled Greene to set novels in such parts of the world as Indochina, Cuba and the Congo shortly before they became centres of global danger and concern.) At all events, the reference is unlikely to be merely casual or accidental. In addition to his taste for parody and pastiche, Greene is a deliberate mystifier and joker. Philip Stratford has shown how Greene is preoccupied with his own name, frequently introducing the proper names 'Greene' or 'Green' into his writing, and being much concerned,

too, with the colour green (and with its conventional chro-
matic opposite, shown in the frequency of names like 'Rose'
or 'Coral').³

In *The Confidential Agent* Greene employs the Flaubertian
counterpoint with considerable subtlety. The context as
well as the song needs to be quoted. At the beginning
of the novel, D., an emissary from the Republicans in
the Spanish Civil War (the country is unnamed but unmistakable), arrives in England on a special mission. At Dover
he meets a rich girl, Rose Cullen, and they drive to London
together. On the way they stop for dinner in a smart
road-house; D.'s enemies are already trying to stop him
and the plot is beginning to develop. The meal is accompanied by a pianist and singer:

> The woman with the deep voice sang an absurd song
> about unrequited love:
>
> > It was just a way of talking—I hadn't learned.
> > It was just day-dreaming—but my heart burned.
> > You said 'I love you'—and I thought you meant it.
> > You said 'My heart is yours'—but you'd only lent it.
>
> People set down their wine and listened as if it were
> poetry. Even the girl stopped eating for a while. The
> self-pity of it irritated him; it was a vice nobody in
> his country on either side of the line had an opportunity
> of indulging.
>
> > I don't say you lie: it's just the modern way.
> > I don't intend to die: in the old Victorian way.
>
> He supposed it represented the 'spirit of the age',
> whatever that meant; he almost preferred the prison
> cell, the law of flight, the bombed house, his enemy
> by the door. He watched the girl moodily; there was
> a time in his life when he would have tried to write
> her a poem—it would have been better stuff than this.
>
> > It was just day-dreaming—I begin to discern it:

It was just a way of talking—and I've started
to learn it.

She said, 'It's muck, isn't it? But it has a sort of
appeal.' (Part I, ch. 1)

The lyric itself is a deft pastiche of the sentimental–cynical
torch song. But in the narrative context it acquires further
implications. For D., whose country is in ruins and whose
wife has been killed in the civil war, the song has no
meaning in itself, and is an index of the futility and unaware-
ness of English life in the late thirties. Rose, realising
little of these matters, claims that the song, however worth-
less, 'has a sort of appeal', like Noël Coward's Amanda
recognising the potency of cheap music. The incident brings
into focus a clash not just of sensibilities but also of historical
circumstances.

It is, however, in *Brighton Rock* that one sees Greene's
interest in popular music most fully indulged. This novel
is like *The Great Gatsby* in containing a rich subtext of
musical references. They are not always used to establish
an ironic Flaubertian contrast. On occasion Greene almost
surrenders to the potency and glamour, however tawdry,
of the music, just as Fitzgerald does. Brighton in summer
is full of music, wafting from the end of the pier.

They were dancing in the open air on the white stone
deck above the Aquarium, and he got down on to the
beach where he was more alone, the dry seaweed left
by last winter's gales cracking under his shoes. He could
hear the music—'The One I Love'. Wrap it up in cello-
phane, he thought, put it in silver paper. (Part IV,
ch. 1)

For the novel's central figure, the lapsed-Catholic teenage
gangster Pinkie, the music is a constant torment, reminding
him of the sexuality that he hates and fears. Even when
he drives out of Brighton to a country road-house he cannot
escape it: 'In the dance hall the band was playing: "Love
me tonight, And forget in daylight, All our delight . . . ." '

These references come to a climax when Pinkie goes to the cinema with the young waitress, Rose, whom he has just married, not out of love but to ensure that she cannot legally testify against him on a murder charge. In this description Greene drew on one of his film reviews. In 1936 he gave a disapproving notice to a musical film, *Rose of the Rancho*, starring a singer called John Boles:

> I find Mr. Boles, his air of confident carnality, the lick of black shiny hair across the plump white waste of face, peculiarly unsympathetic; and never more so than in this film as he directs his lick, his large assured amorous eyes, towards Miss Swarthout and croons:
>
> > I call you a gift from the angels,
> > For I feel in my heart you're divine.[4]

In the novel the account becomes more ambivalent as it is transformed into Pinkie's own confused response:

> The two main characters made their stately progress towards the bed sheets: 'I loved you that first time in Santa Monica . . . .' A song under the window, a girl in a nightdress and the clock beside the screen moving on. He whispered suddenly, furiously, to Rose: 'Like cats.' It was the commonest game under the sun— why be scared at what the dogs did in the streets? The music moaned—'I know in my heart you're divine.' . . . The actor with a lick of black hair across a white waste of face said, 'You're mine, All mine.' He sang again under the restless stars in a wash of incredible moonshine, and suddenly, inexplicably, the Boy began to weep. He shut his eyes to hold in his tears, but the music went on—it was like a vision of release to an imprisoned man. He felt constriction and saw—hopelessly out of reach—a limitless freedom: no fear, no hatred, no envy. It was as if he were dead and were remembering the effect of a good confession, the words of absolution: but being dead it was a memory only—he couldn't experience contrition—the ribs of his body were like steel bands

which held him down to eternal unrepentance. He said at last: 'Let's go. We'd better go'. (Part VI, ch. 2)

As Rose and Pinkie walk away from the cinema, 'A wail of music came off the sea.' Earlier, Pinkie has reacted to Rose in one of Greene's characteristically far-fetched similes: 'the possible depths of her fidelity touched him like cheap music'. The echo from the totally other world of Coward's Elyot and Amanda could be deliberate.

In this novel, too, Greene inserts a lyric. The occasion is when Pinkie takes Rose, whom he has not yet married, to a dance hall:

A spotlight picked out a patch of floor, a crooner in a dinner jacket, a microphone on a long black movable stand. He held it tenderly as if it were a woman, swinging it gently this way and that, wooing it with his lips while from the loudspeaker under the gallery his whisper reverberated hoarsely over the hall, like a dictator announcing victory, like the official news following a long censorship. 'It gets you,' the Boy said, 'it gets you,' surrendering himself to the huge brazen suggestion.

Music talks, talks of our love.
The starling on our walks, talks, talks of our love.
The taxis tooting,
The last owl hooting,
The tube train rumbling,
Busy bee bumbling,
    Talk of our love.

Music talks, talks of our love,
The west wind on our walks, talks of our love.
The nightingale singing,
The postman ringing,
Electric drill groaning,
Office telephoning,
    Talk of our love.

> The watchdog on our walks, talks, talks of
>   our love . . .
> Gracie Fields funning,
> The gangsters gunning,
>   Talk of our love.   (Part II, ch. 1)

The introductory paragraph offers a precise sense of period,
though the imagery is Greene's rather than Pinkie's. In
the late thirties dictators and crooners were both components
of the scene; and both used microphones. The lyric itself
is a good parody of the popular catalogue songs of the
time, like 'You're the Top' or 'These Foolish Things'.
Although not now critically assessing Greene's early fiction,
I must remark that on rereading *Brighton Rock* I find it
much better than I once did. Critics have dismissed this
book as a confused mixture of a thriller, a realistic story
of Brighton low life and a theological fable; but these
multiple dimensions now seem to me a source of strength
rather than weakness. It may be that we had to wait
to get accustomed to the fiction of deliberately mixed genres
that emerged in the sixties and seventies before we could
learn to read *Brighton Rock* properly.

Greene's novels of the years from 1932 to 1939 form
a clearly defined phase. In 1940, with *The Power and the
Glory*, he entered a new one. He extended his settings
from pre-war Europe to remoter and more transparently
violent parts of the world—Mexico, West Africa, Indochina,
the Congo—whilst concentrating more exclusively on the
drama of the individual human soul. Greene's fictional
action became intensive rather than extensive. This is noticeable in his presentation of wartime and post-war London
in *The End of the Affair*, which lacks the cinematic range
and knowing social observation of his novels of the thirties.
And his treatment in successive novels of the religious themes
first raised in *Brighton Rock* meant that for several years
Greene, to his embarrassment and annoyance, was primarily
known as a 'Catholic novelist'. After 1939 Greene largely
gave up introducing snatches of popular songs into his
novels. He continued to quote and allude, but to more
reputably literary material, like the passages from Rilke

in *The Ministry of Fear* and *The Heart of the Matter*. In
the thirties Greene had inventively used the popular song,
just as he had used the conventions of other popular arts,
like the thriller and the cinema, which were so much
part of the consciousness of the time, and which interested
many other writers. Unlike his contemporaries, though,
Greene was never an explicitly political writer; and he
had not yet appeared to be an explicitly religious one.
If he registered the prevalent sense of crisis and threat
of war, particularly in *A Gun for Sale* and *The Confidential
Agent*, he was more immediately concerned to present sharply
but selectively the socio-cultural characteristics of urban
life in the thirties. In one sense, Greene is remarkably
open to typical cultural experience, just like the good
reporter who was so much a cult figure of the period.
At the same time, he is an intensely idiosyncratic—indeed,
obsessional—writer, who sees and records what is significant
to him. It is in this respect that Greene reproduces, ironically
but still affectionately, the popular songs that had become
an omnipresent expression of collective experience. His re-
creation of them has something in common with what would
later be known, in another medium, as pop art. In a
literal sense, they meant something to him. In Greene's
own versions of these songs we see a nice example of
the intersection of the typical and the personal.

7 Icon or Commodity?

During the thirties cinemas were built all over Britain, spreading an illusion of luxury and splendour in the midst of slump and mass unemployment. In A. J. P. Taylor's words,

> Glittering cinema palaces went up everywhere, even in the most impoverished areas. In Liverpool it was calculated, 40 per cent of the population went to the cinema once a week, 25 per cent went twice. The cinema was church and theatre in one, though with no communal reality.[1]

In *The Dog Beneath the Skin* Auden observed

> ... the cinema blazing with bulbs: bowers of bliss
> Where thousands are holding hands: they gape at
> the tropical vegetation, at the Ionic pillars and
> the organ solo.

Comments on the attractions and ritual of film-going are common in the literature of the time, though authorial attitudes varied from the mocking distaste of Lewis Grassic Gibbon in *Grey Granite* to acceptance of the glamorous spectacle in Graham Greene's *Brighton Rock* and *The Confidential Agent*. Both these writers noted a recurring *topos* of the contemporary cinema. 'The film did a sudden close-up of her face with a tear of gratitude two feet long trembling like a jelly from her lower eyelid' (*Grey Granite*). 'There was a lot of suffering—gelatine tears pouring down the big blonde features—and a lot of happiness' (*The Confidential Agent*). The poets were equally concerned. In 'Newsreel', Day Lewis wrote of the cinema audience,

> Fish in their tank electrically heated
> Nose without envy the glass wall: for them
> Clerk, spy, nurse, killer, prince, the great and the
>   defeated,
> Move in a mute day-dream.

Even Dylan Thomas, a poet whose preoccupations were visceral rather than social, produced these sharp lines (in 'Our Eunuch Dreams'):

> In this our age the gunman and his moll,
> Two one-dimensional ghosts, love on a reel,
> Strange to our solid eye,
> And speak their midnight nothings as they swell;
> When cameras shut they hurry to their hole
> Down in the yard of day.
>
> They dance between their arclamps and our skull,
> Impose their shots, throwing the nights away;
> We watch the show of shadows kiss or kill,
> Flavoured of celluloid give love the lie.

The cinemas provided, for the price of a ticket, temporary sensations of very gracious living, with warmth, soft lights, deep carpets, the sweet music of the organ, all enclosed by a truly palatial architecture. Louis MacNeice wrote in 'Eclogue from Iceland':

> C. What is that music in the air—
>   Organ-music coming from afar?
>
> R. Honeyed-music—it sounds to me
>   Like the Wurlitzer in the Gaiety.
>
> G. I do not hear anything at all.

C. Imagine the purple light on the stage

R. The melting moment of a stinted age

C. The pause before the film again
   Bursts in a shower of golden rain.

MacNeice, a professional classicist, would have been deliberately alluding to Zeus, who appeared to the imprisoned
Danae in a shower of golden rain. The film could manifest
a godlike power and the cinema was a temple as well
as a picture-palace. Or, to put it a little differently, the
cinema was a shrine for the worship of the super-stars.
Gavin Ewart, in his 'Verse from an Opera' from *Poems
and Songs* (1938), introduced some of them in a secular
litany of the saints that parodies a Cole Porter catalogue
song:

> Is it Maurice's hat
> Or a furnished flat
>   That makes your pulses beat?
> Is your paradise
> In Garbo's eyes
>   Or Ginger Rogers' feet?
>
> Is it Colman's smile
> That makes life worth while
>   Or Crawford's significant form?
> Is it Lombard's lips
> Or Mae West's hips
>   That carry you through the storm?

At the end of *Autumn Journal* MacNeice brought into sardonic
apposition the super-stars and the major intellectual influences of the age:

> Sleep quietly, Marx and Freud,
>   The figure-heads of our transition.
> Cagney, Lombard, Bing and Garbo,
>   Sleep in your world of celluloid.

Of all the stars, Garbo was the most often referred to, by poets and novelists and the writers of popular songs. Auden linked her name with Cleopatra's in 'O for doors to be open and an invite with gilded edges' (Poem XXIV of *Look, Stranger!*). Strachey, Link and Marvell made Garbo's smile one of These Foolish Things that Remind Me of You:

> The smile of Garbo and the scent of roses,
> The waiter's whistle as the last bar closes.

Less sentimentally, Cole Porter took a quasi-Marxist view of Garbo in 'You're the Top', where she embodies fetishistic economic value, ironically related by rhyme to a great repository of high culture:

> You're the National Gallery,
> You're Garbo's salary . . . .

A. S. J. Tessimond, in 'Steel April' (published in *New Country*), presented Garbo as one more fragmented image of a collapsing society:

> You say that our civilisation is hasty incompetent
>   filing;
> a Tiller troupe filling its gaps from the ranks of
>   the spare Pavlovas;
> a musical-comedy chorus of newsboys and opera
>   singers;
> Hollywood framing the face of Garbo and
>   sex-for-hicks.

From the beginning, 'Garbo' had many implications. Evelyn Waugh was, throughout his life, a frequent film-goer, and in *Vile Bodies* he provides an early reference to Garbo. This novel is, as Samuel Hynes has pointed out in *The Auden Generation*, closer than most of Waugh's fiction to the social and political preoccupations of the thirties; newspapers and films form prominent subtexts in the narrative. Colonel Blount is a great enthusiast for the cinema, as he explains to his prospective son-in-law, Adam Fenwick-Symes:

> 'I was looking at some of the houses they're putting up outside Aylesbury. Did you see them coming along? Nice little red houses. Bathroom and everything. Quite cheap, too, and near the cinematographs. I hope you are fond of the cinematograph too? The Rector and I go a great deal. I hope you'll like the Rector. Common little man rather. But he's got a motor-car, useful that. How long are you staying?'
> 'I promised Nina I'd be back to-night.'
> 'That's a pity. They change the film at the Electra Palace. We might have gone.'
> An elderly woman servant came in to announce luncheon.
> 'What is at the Electra Palace, do you know, Mrs. Florin?'
> 'Greta Garbo in *Venetian Kisses*, I think, Sir.'
> 'I don't really think I like Greta Garbo, I've tried to,' said Colonel Blount, 'but I just don't.'   (Ch. 5)

A few years later the shabby hero of George Orwell's *Keep the Aspidistra Flying* observes the tawdry glamour of a London picture-palace where a Garbo film is showing. Gordon Comstock is a depressed and embittered poet who regards the cinema as all too successfully rivalling literature as a purveyor of drama:

> Gordon halted outside a great garish picture-house, under the weary eye of the commissionaire, to examine the photographs. Greta Garbo in *The Painted Veil*. He yearned to go inside, not for Greta's sake, but just for the warmth and the softness of the velvet seat. He hated the pictures, of course, seldom went there even when he could afford it. Why encourage the art that is destined to replace literature? But still, there is a kind of soggy attraction about it. To sit on the padded seat in the warm smoke-scented darkness, letting the flickering drivel on the screen gradually overwhelm you—feeling the waves of its silliness

lap you round till you seem to drown, intoxicated, in a viscous sea—after all, it's the kind of drug we need. The right drug for friendless people. (Ch. 4)

A character in Lawrence Durrell's *The Black Book* refers to 'that Swedish maneater, Greta Garbo'. Her manifestations seemed endless; she was a metonymic emblem of the star-system or even the cinema itself.

More diffusedly, she was an embodiment of cultural and personal style throughout the thirties; even, on occasion, part of the furniture. In a first novel of 1934, Barbara Lucas's *Stars Were Born* (appearing in the same list as Jean Rhys's *Voyage in the Dark*), a young woman, just married and set up in a studio in Fitzroy Square, has a picture of Garbo on the mantelpiece as a matter of course. In Anthony Powell's *Agents and Patients* we find this description of Berlin:

Sitting in the Romanisches Café they looked out, as from the bastion of a neo-gothic fort, at the crowd. A steady stream of dolled-up girls—Dietrich, Garbo and Harvey the prevalent styles—passed underneath the café's parapet and crossed towards the spiky grey church or to the other corner where a stunted Nazi with galloping consumption was selling newspapers. (Ch. 4)

(At that time in Germany Garbo's celebrity was rivalled by Marlene Dietrich and Lilian Harvey.) Among the constant flicker of observations of urban scenery in Graham Greene's *Brighton Rock* occurs this sentence: 'They turned up through Norfolk Square towards Montpelier Road: a blonde with Garbo cheeks paused to powder on the steps up to the Norfolk bar.' In Greene's *England Made Me* we find such references as 'a girl with hair like Greta Garbo's, walking alone', and ' "I love the sea," the blonde said, with Garbo in her voice.' The Garbo image was capable of endless replication, by the films in which she starred, by photographs, and ultimately by her effect on fashion and the ideals of feminine style.

There are some pertinent sentences in Walter Benjamin's

famous essay 'The Work of Art in the Age of Mechanical Reproduction', originally published in 1936. Benjamin does not mention Garbo by name, but he discusses the star-system in Marxist terms as an elaborate form of commodity fetishism:

> The feeling of strangeness that overcomes the actor before the camera, as Pirandello describes it, is basically of the same kind as the estrangement felt before one's own image in the mirror. But now the reflected image has become separable, transportable. And where is it transported? Before the public. Never for a moment does the screen actor cease to be conscious of this fact. While facing the camera he knows that ultimately he will face the public, the consumers who constitute the market. This market, where he offers not only his labor but also his whole self, his heart and soul, is beyond his reach. During the shooting he has as little contact with it as any article made in a factory. This may contribute to that oppression, that new anxiety which, according to Pirandello, grips the actor before the camera. The film responds to the shriveling of the aura with an artificial build-up of the 'personality' outside the studio. The cult of the movie star, fostered by the money of the film industry, preserves not the unique aura of the person but the 'spell of the personality', the phony spell of a commodity.[2]

It is indeed possible to see Garbo as a reified commodity, a dehumanised product of the Hollywood dream factory. But such an analysis, though relevant, is ultimately reductive, since it fails to account for the particularity of the appeal: why did *this* particular face become so compelling an image, to the cinema-going public and to writers? (Benjamin's thesis is better illustrated, I think, in cruder instances, like the truly totalitarian multiplication of Ruby Keeler's winsome features until they fill the whole screen—like those of Führer or Duce—to the accompaniment of 'I Only Have Eyes for You', in the Busby Berkeley musical *Dames*). Something of a unique personality *was* conveyed, despite the 'shrivelling' effect of the movie machine.

Mechanical replication is one axis; uniqueness of personality is another, and the point of intersection may be called the iconic. The Mona Lisa is the most celebrated of all instances of what I would regard as an iconic portrait. It is pervaded with mystery, with the sense of a unique if elusive personality; and at the same time, as Benjamin remarks, it was constantly copied, long before the age of mechanical reproduction. More than any other writer of the thirties, Graham Greene was aware of the iconic aspect of Garbo. In *England Made Me,* in addition to the passing references mentioned above, Garbo makes an unnamed but unmistakable personal appearance. The setting is Stockholm, and the observer is Minty, a down-at-heel, expatriate English journalist, watching from a café opposite the station:

On the point of opening one of the letters he paused, his eye caught by an unusual activity at the station. Several men were running across the road with movie cameras. He saw Nils darting by outside and waved to him. He remembered what it was all about. 'The film star's return home.' He had earned sixty crowns a few days ago translating into Swedish all the dope he could discover in the movie magazines. 'The screen's greatest lover.' 'The mystery woman of Hollywood.' A number of people (were they hired by the hour? Minty wondered) began to cheer, and several business men, with portfolios under their arms, stopped on the pavement and scowled at the station. They obscured Minty's view. Minty stood on his chair. It was just as well to keep an eye open even if it was not his own pigeon. The actress was not very popular in Sweden; something disgraceful might happen; something which someone would want hushed up. If, for example, she was hissed . . . . .

But nothing happened. A woman came out of the station in a camel-hair coat with a big collar; it was just possible to see that she was wearing grey flannel trousers; Minty had one glimpse of a pale haggard humourless face, a long upper lip, the unreal loveliness

and the unreal tragedy of a mask like Dante's known
too well. The movie cameras whirred and the woman
put her hands in front of her face and stepped into
a car. Somebody threw an expensive bouquet of flowers
(who paid for that? Minty wondered) which missed the
car and fell in the road. Nobody took any notice. A
little woman in heavy black tweeds and a black veil
scuttled into the car and it drove away. The newspaper-
men came together in front of the station and Minty
could hear their laughter.   (Part III, ch. 1)

In his film reviews Greene admired Garbo as an actress
but complained that she generally appeared in boring and
inadequate vehicles. His review of *Anna Karenina*, published
in *The Spectator* on 11 October 1935, recalls the description
in *England Made Me* (on other occasions Greene's film
reviews were a source for references in his novels, but
here the fictional account seems to have come first):

What beauty she has is harsh and austere as an Arab's;
and I was reminded of Mr. Yeats's lines on Dante's
mask:

An image that might have been a stony face,
Staring upon a bedouin's horse-hair roof
From doored and windowed cliff, or half upturned
Among the coarse grass and the camel dung.[3]

The Yeats lines come from 'Ego Dominus Tuus', a profound
but difficult meditation on the polarities of image and
reality, self and anti-self, mask and face. By this comparison
Greene assimilated Garbo to a central modernist tradition,
of aloof, mask-like, iconic beauty. Pater on the Mona Lisa
is a famous early example; in this century there was Eliot's
praise of the revue comedienne Ethel Levey as 'the most
aloof and impersonal of personalities'.[4]
    In the 1950s Roland Barthes elaborated the iconography
of Garbo in a short essay, 'The Face of Garbo', where
he remarks on her mask-like beauty in *Queen Christina*:
'Garbo offered to one's gaze a sort of Platonic Idea of

the human creature, which explains why her face is almost sexually undefined, without however leaving one in doubt.' Barthes concludes with a familiar kind of binary opposition: 'Viewed as a transition the face of Garbo reconciles two iconographic ages, it assures the passage from awe to charm.' The nearer pole of this opposition is represented by Audrey Hepburn: 'The face of Garbo is an Idea, that of Hepburn, an Event.'[6] Whilst Benjamin defines the star as a commodity, Barthes projects her—this star, at least—as an icon. Traditionally, the ideal beauty of the icon or anti-self depended on an hieratic or aristocratic art and scheme of values; but Garbo was the creation of the cinema, a mass medium whose images were capable of unlimited multiplication and distribution to the largest and least differentiated audience in history. It is a paradox that remains arresting; in the thirties its implications would have been particularly evident to practitioners of the threatened art of literature.

8 Conclusion

I

I have not said very much about the politics of the thirties, and this may seem a major omission to some readers. But the subject has already been well treated by other writers, particularly by Samuel Hynes in *The Auden Generation*, which is subtitled 'Literature and Politics in England in the 1930s'. I have, rather, wanted to draw attention to other and less discussed contexts, which seem to me at least as important as the political. Nevertheless, there is one topic I should like to touch on briefly before trying to draw some general conclusions from the preceding chapters. In a vigorous and provocative article published in *Encounter* in 1973, George Watson argued that the left-wing intellectuals of the thirties were not ignorant dupes of Communism, as is now generally assumed, but knowing and deliberate supporters, not only of Marxist theory, but also of the whole apparatus of Stalinist terror.[1] Watson's charges were attacked by survivors of the thirties and defended by him, in a subsequent correspondence that ran over several months. His essay is certainly damaging, though my ultimate response is that it is too much a case for the prosecution and too little of a disinterested enquiry into intellectual history. Without doubt uncomfortable facts about Soviet Russia were available in England in the thirties, though the intellectuals of the time were too blinded by ideology to want to know anything about them. Humankind cannot bear too much reality, or fight on too many fronts at once. For the left-wing writers of the thirties, the immediate, inescapable reality was that capitalism seemed to be collapsing, as evidenced by slump and mass unemployment and general misery in the Western democracies, and the triumph of fascism—seen in Marxist terms as the ultimate, most vicious form of capitalism—in Italy and Germany. Soviet Russia claimed to offer the only hope for humanity, and its claims were accepted, unhesitatingly, at their face value. Repression and the destruction of human life in Soviet Russia were, of course, on a much larger scale than anything that happened in Nazi Germany, at least until the Second World War (not until the Final Solution did Hitler begin to catch up with Stalin).[2] But very few intellectuals—Orwell, after his return from Spain was one of them—had the independence and courage to be equally opposed to fascism and Communism. Instead, a simplistic, sentimental Russophilia was pervasive: one finds it, for instance, in the pages of *Left Review*, where the sharpness of the anti-capitalist polemic is in striking contrast to the naivety of the pro-Soviet propaganda. The Russophilia died down with the Hitler–Stalin pact in 1939, then revived on an enormous scale after Germany invaded Russia in 1941. It is still far from extinct in quarters of the English Left.

Much can be ascribed to extreme gullibility, even criminal folly. But what of George Watson's claim that thirties writers were knowing upholders of terror and massacre? It needs, I think, more extensive documentation than he supplies, but it should be taken seriously. After all, some of the most admired and heroic figures who fought in the International Brigades, as refugees from Eastern Europe, were ten or fifteen years later acting as the ruthless agents of Stalinist repression in their own countries. Certain English Communist intellectuals—Cornford, Fox, Caudwell—fought and were killed and are remembered as martyrs. Given a different turn of fate and history they might have survived as diligent members of the Politbureau of an English Soviet Republic. There is no reason to suppose that British Communists were inherently less tough-minded than their European comrades. Thus, Stephen Spender observes in *World*

Within World,

> Indeed I have never ceased to be astonished by the
> extent to which Communists are indifferent to awkward
> facts. For example, one day I asked Chalmers what
> he thought of the most recent Moscow trials in which
> Yagoda, who had been largely responsible for incriminat-
> ing the victims of the previous purge, had himself been
> sentenced to death. Chalmers looked up, with his bright
> glance like a bird-watcher's, and said: 'What trials? I've
> given up thinking about such things ages ago.'
>
> What he really meant, I suppose, was that having
> chosen to be a Communist by an act of will, he now
> admitted no point of view which was inconvenient to
> the Party. The dictatorship of the proletariat did not
> pretend to be bourgeois justice. Stalin had only to decide
> that someone was an enemy for him to become one.
> To criticize (except within the Party) what the Party
> did was to put oneself on 'the wrong side of history'.[3]

The egregious Hugh MacDiarmid, writer of two 'Hymns
to Lenin' in the thirties, actually rejoined the Communist
Party as a sign of his support for the Soviet invasion
of Hungary in 1956, when many of its most idealistic
members were leaving it.

George Watson argues that Spender himself was a knowing
supporter of Stalinist terror in the thirties, on the basis
of sentences quoted from his *Forward From Liberalism*. They
can support that interpretation, but the book as a whole
does not. Read with normal literary-critical attention to
tone and feeling, it appears as the work of someone desperately trying to convince himself of the truth of what he
is saying. Even as a new convert to Communism, Spender
allowed himself doubts about the conduct of the Moscow
trials, and for this he was sharply criticised by Harry
Pollitt, the leader of the British Communist Party. Spender
himself soon disowned *Forward From Liberalism*. It is one
of the texts of the time that illustrate the melancholy
paradox that literary men, when seized by political passions,
can often use words without knowing what they mean.

'Terror', 'killing', 'dictatorship' could be seen as disagreeable but temporary manifestations of the transitional aspect of the Soviet system (with the implication that the numbers involved ran into a few hundred instead of, as we now know, many millions). It is a way of using words from the top of the head, so to speak, or, in Newman's distinction, with a notional rather than a real assent. This, of course, was the charge laid by George Orwell in his crucial essay on the thirties, 'Inside the Whale', where he attacks Auden's 'Spain' for the lines

> Today the deliberate increase in the chances of
>   death,
> The conscious acceptance of guilt in the necessary
>   murder . . . .

This, Orwell remarks, could only have been written 'by a person to whom murder is at most a *word*'. (George Watson dissents from Orwell, insisting that Auden could well have meant it, and been in favour of political murder.) As we know, Auden was very unhappy about the phrase. He later changed 'necessary murder' to the 'fact of murder', then eventually excluded the whole poem from his corpus. The point is surely that the use of 'murder' at all points to evasiveness and uncertainty on Auden's part. It is pacifist rhetoric in a fighting context. That is to say, if one believes that a war in defence of the Spanish Republic is justified— which is what 'Spain' is saying—then killing the enemy in that war will be necessary if disagreeable. One should then speak of 'necessary killing' or 'necessary homicide'. Pacifists believe that war is never justified, and that all killing in war is 'murder'. By using this word Auden, in effect, undermines his own cause. In fact, 'Spain' is a very detached and equivocal poem, considering the degree of feeling that the Civil War aroused. It has nothing of the lyrical passion of Neruda's 'España en el Corazón'; or, to take an example from the other side, Claudel's 'Aux Martyrs Espagnols'.

For a long time the Auden of the thirties has been conventionally regarded as a political, committed poet writing with an end in view, and some of his early poems, such as 'A Communist to Others' (published under that title in *New Country* in 1933; collected in a shorter version as Poem XIV of *Look, Stranger!*; dropped from *Collected Shorter Poems*), support that judgement. Yet recent evidence from Christopher Isherwood may revise that opinion. Early in 1939 he and Auden were sailing together to America:

> Now, communication between them was re-established. This, to Christopher at least, meant an unaccustomed freedom. Alone with Wystan, he was able, literally, to speak his mind—to say things which he hadn't known were in it, until the moment of speaking. One morning, when they were walking on the deck, Christopher heard himself say: 'You know, it just doesn't mean anything to me any more—the Popular Front, the party line, the anti-fascist struggle. I suppose they're okay but something's wrong with me. I simply cannot swallow another mouthful.' To which Wystan answered: 'Neither can I'.
>
> Those were not their exact words, but, psychologically, it was as simple as that. They had been playing parts, repeating slogans created for them by others. Now they wanted to stop. Christopher felt almost equally surprised by his own statement and by Wystan's agreement with it. The surprise was mutual. Their agreement made them happy.[4]

After calling for 'a change of heart' in the 1930 *Poems*, Auden had had a further change by 1939, leading him away from politics and collectivism to religion and individualism.

The relations of literature and politics at that time were evident and interesting. The other ways in which the texts of literature and the texts of history intersected were less immediately apparent, and I have tried to indicate some of them in the preceding chapters. Frontiers and spies, bombers and the threat of war, were facts of the age, a palpable part of public consciousness; in literature they occurred not only as signifiers of an external reality but also as metaphors and recurring formal constituents. But history was not merely politics and economics and opposed nationalisms; it also implied cultural and social changes on a very large scale. And these changes were independent of ideological or national differences. In particular, I am thinking of the impact of technological mass culture on traditional high culture. As we have seen, in the years before 1914 the Futurists welcomed and celebrated the machine age, and it is surely significant that in the twenties Marinetti, an Italian Futurist, became a Fascist, while Mayakovski, a Russian Futurist, became a Communist. England was culturally conservative, but by the early thirties it was apparent that mass civilisation had arrived and was threatening traditional values. This was the message of F. R. Leavis's early pamphlet *Mass Civilization and Minority Culture*, which drew urgent, strongly disapproving attention to the effect of the cinema, the radio and mass-circulation newspapers. As I have remarked in an earlier chapter, the basic technology of the motor-car, the aeroplane, the cinema and the radio existed before 1914 (not to mention that early nineteenth-century invention the locomotive), but their cultural significance as modes of mass communication was not really apparent, at least in England, until the early thirties. Leavis summed up what we now call the 'mass media' as an invading 'Americanism' and he was right to do so; the European avant-garde had long admired the America—an ideal or imaginary construction in many cases—of mass culture and advanced technology, whilst English cultural conservatives deplored it. But the facts were not in dispute. In 1930, the year in which Leavis's pamphlet appeared, the advance of Americanism was given a powerful boost by the arrival of the talking films. I have looked in previous chapters at the way in which writers were interested in the cinema and the popular song. Another technological advance in mass culture that was frequently reflected in the literature of the thirties was the transformation of urban landscape at night by electric advertising signs. Here are three examples.

> High in the air, in empty space,
> Five times a minute a mug is filled

> And in ten-foot letters, time after time,
> Words are spelt out and wiped away.
>   (Auden and Isherwood, *The Dog Beneath the Skin*)

He watched the skysigns flicking on and off, glaring red and blue, arrowing up and down—the awful, sinister glitter of a doomed civilization, like the still blazing lights of a sinking ship.
>   (Orwell, *Keep the Aspidistra Flying*)

> Nelson is stone and Johnnie Walker moves his
> Legs like a cretin over Trafalgar Square.
>   (MacNeice, *Autumn Journal*)

Orwell's distaste is extreme; in general the tone is informed but unenthusiastic. What one does not find is the romanticism with which the *fin de siècle* poets regarded the gas-lit streets of London ('the iron lilies of the Strand'), or the ebullience with which the Futurists might have greeted such vivid transformations of the familiar. (One may compare the enthusiasm with which a present-day American cultural commentator, Tom Wolfe, has described the overwhelming lights of Las Vegas.[5])

The poets and novelists of the thirties were observant, taking careful note of the cultural changes visible all around them: not for nothing was the keen-eyed, hard-headed reporter a hero in the films and popular fiction of the time. Novelists looked closely at urban life and landscape—in ways partly learnt from the cinema—and poets, who had been shown by Eliot that there are no inherently unpoetic subjects, tried to be as observant as novelists. But to observe is one thing, to respond another. After early attempts at a positive response, as suggested in Auden's salute to 'new styles of architecture' or Spender's neo-Futurist praise of pylons and aeroplanes and locomotives (somewhat paralleled in America by Hart Crane's *The Bridge*) enthusiasm for the new technology becomes harder to maintain; the pressures of English literary tradition, tending to the rural, the anti-urban and the anti-technological, were increasingly felt. And there were some aspects of mass civilisation in the thirties that the writers of the time could not contemplate with anything other than profound distaste. I mean the spread of dormitory suburbs around our large cities, and the prevalence, in particular, of mock-Tudor styles of architecture. As MacNeice wrote in 'Birmingham':

Splayed outwards through the suburbs houses, houses
    for rest
Seducingly rigged by the builder, half-timbered
    houses with lips pressed
So tightly and eyes staring at the traffic through
    bleary haws
And only a six-inch grip of the racing earth in
    their concrete claws . . . .

Derision of the new suburb and in particular of the half-timbered villa is a constantly recurring literary motif. For instance, in Graham Greene's *A Gun for Sale* there is a precise but horrified description of a suburban housing estate under construction. It is true that the new suburbs offered nothing that could appeal to either progressive or conservative intellectuals. They lacked the technological smartness of the products of the Bauhaus, as well as the decent spaciousness of the sort of houses—those of the professional classes—in which most English literary men had grown up and in which they reckoned to live themselves. All the same, millions of English people appreciated them, finding in the new suburbs a far pleasanter mode of living than they had known in the inner city; even the bogus half-timbering of the 'Tudorbethan' style and the tiny patches of garden, so uniformly mocked by the intellectuals, were an emblem, however pathetic, of the Englishman's perennial aspiration to live like a country yeoman. These were the kinds of houses that the English inconsiderately preferred to the new workers' flats of Russia or Weimar Germany, much admired in progressive circles. It has been left to subsequent architectural historians—notably J. M. Richards in *Castles on the Ground* (1946; second edition, 1973) and Alan A. Jackson in *Semi-Detached London*

(1973)—to write about between-wars suburbia with the sympathetic interest that the poets and novelists lacked.

As a description of the literary situation of the thirties, the title of Leavis's pamphlet offers an apt polarity: 'mass civilisation' as against 'minority culture'. The writers I have been discussing were very much products of 'minority culture', as represented in the specialised humanistic training of the public school, and the cultivated family background of the educated upper middle class. And in some of them rural nostalgia, so characteristic of English polite culture, was conspicuous from the beginning. Day Lewis writes, for instance, in 'Letter to a Young Revolutionary',

> And now, the country at last. Past factories, sports grounds, tame rusticity of 'garden cities,' bogus Elizabethan villas, petrol stations disguised as mosques, chapels like mausoleums and amusement parks like death. The country at last. And a poor enough outlook it is. Stunted crops, derelict barns, mills deserted to rats, good land given over to sheep and golfers. Somebody has run away. In the rectory the rector is reading Jeans or practising string tricks for the next village entertainment. Listen to the children, as we walk past the school, chanting in unison the kings of England and the capitals of Europe, their birthright of natural wisdom exchanged for a mess of knowledge. And the parents? The backbone of the country? The marrow seems to have been drained off. Can these dry bones live? Can they live on the tinned foods, cheap cigarettes, votes, synthetic pearls, jazz records and standardised clothing which the town gives them back, as a 'civilised' trader gives savages beads for gold? They damn well can't, and you know it. And it's up to you, if you want to see the country sound again, to put its heart back in the right place, even though it means what the progress-mongers call 'putting the clock back'. You must break up the superficial vision of the motorist and restore the slow, instinctive, absorbent vision of the countryman. Not exile mind, intellectual consciousness; but stop it trespassing in other fields. The land must be a land of milk and honey, of crops and

cattle, not a string of hotels and 'beauty spots'. Can your revolution do something about all this? If not, I've no use for it.[6]

Similar things were said by Lawrence and Eliot and Leavis, and were later picked up by Orwell in 'Inside the Whale':

To say 'I accept' in an age like our own is to say that you accept concentration camps, rubber truncheons, Hitler, Stalin, bombs, aeroplanes, tinned food, machine-guns, putsches, purges, slogans, Bedaux belts, gasmasks, submarines, spies, *provocateurs*, press censorship, secret prisons, aspirins, Hollywood films and political murders.[7]

Orwell is generally and rightly regarded as a conspicuously honest writer, but in this passage his rhetoric is surely dishonest. He is giving mass civilisation a damningly bad name by identifying all of it with its most atrocious political and technological manifestations. Looking dispassionately at Orwell's list one can say that some items—aeroplanes, tinned food and Hollywood films—are not self-evidently bad and are arguably good. And it is certainly perverse of Orwell to include aspirins on his list, considering how much they have done to alleviate human suffering. In Day Lewis's dismissal of 'jazz records' and Orwell's of 'Hollywood films' there is a similar inability to come to terms with the characteristic aesthetic products of mass civilisation, or, if you prefer, of 'Americanism'. The inability was not general: Graham Greene, for instance, as I have shown, was sympathetic to both jazz and films. But the pattern recurs throughout the thirties: the observation, often in a sharp, particularising, typifying way; then the difficulty of responding, of understanding and judging. These writers, as I see them, were the first literary generation in England to have to face mass civilisation directly, though with a sensibility formed by traditional, minority culture. That encounter, or that frontier, is, I believe, a major determinant of the literature of the time.[8]

II

Some writers were more important than others, and I
shall conclude by saying who I think they were, having
devoted so much of my time to tracing structures rather
than making judgements. In terms of both influence and
accomplishment Auden remains central, though I believe
that he became less interesting as a poet after the mid-thir-
ties, and less interesting still after he went to America,
which is not to say that I dismiss his middle and later
periods out of hand. For me the peak of the achievement
is in *Look, Stranger!* and the poetic sections of *The Orators*
and *The Dog Beneath the Skin*. There Auden's very individual
vision and tone were in balance with his capacity for
general statement and taking large views of things, whether
conceptual or geographical. But it was not an easy balance
to maintain. Throughout the period, though, Auden
remained a dazzling verbal performer. Few English poets
have equalled Auden's skill as a virtuoso of language, and
very few have surpassed him. And as performance his poems
can satisfy for a long time. Yet against the skill and brilliance
one must set evasiveness and the obscurity that arises from
it, and, more profoundly still, one's sense of a lack of
centre in Auden's poetic persona. The clue to that, about
which more is now becoming known, may well lie in
Auden's homosexuality, of which Isherwood has remarked,
'Wystan was much more apologetic about his homosexuality
than Christopher was, and much less aggressive. His religion
condemned it and he agreed that it was sinful, though
he fully intended to go on sinning.'[9]

MacNeice was a simpler poet and, in an absolute sense,
less gifted than Auden. But his work of the thirties wears
uncommonly well, whether it takes the form of songs or
philosophical reflection or ironic social commentary. In Mac-
Neice the centre of personality is palpably there, variously
witty and sentimental and nostalgic. And, though a man
of the Left, he was detached enough to give no hostages
to fortune in the form of ideological commitment, and
his poetry requires little historical justification. Teaching
an undergraduate course on the 1930s, I found that students

who were intrigued but puzzled by Auden could respond
at once, and very positively, to MacNeice, particularly
to *Autumn Journal*. That is not the only test of poetic
quality, of course, but it is still a test. To speak for myself
I find the appeal of *Autumn Journal* almost inexhaustible;
I think it one of the outstanding achievements of the thirties;
indeed, one of the few unremittingly good long poems
in English of this century. It is as unflinchingly personal
as the confessional poetry that came to be so much admired
in the 1960s, whilst being the work of a man who is
well aware of the society he lives in, and sees himself
as inescapably involved with history at a time of public
crisis and threatening war. And, unlike later poets of committed subjectivity, MacNeice does not assume that one must
abandon one's intelligence in order to write personally.
Throughout the poem MacNeice uses contemporary idioms
and images and codes to express very personal meanings,
notably in the passages of love poetry.

Amongst novels of the thirties one of those that I most
admire was written by a man who was twenty years older
than the Auden generation and who had long been well
known if not much liked as a literary personality. It is
Wyndham Lewis's *The Revenge for Love*, in which Lewis
looks sardonically at the political preoccupations of his
juniors and in which crossing a frontier plays an important
part in the plot. Books by younger novelists, born early
in this century, that I enjoy and value include Evelyn
Waugh's *Decline and Fall*, *Vile Bodies* and *A Handful of
Dust*, and Anthony Powell's *Afternoon Men* and *From a View
to a Death*. But Waugh and Powell, though sharing the
experience of the Auden generation because of their age
and education, were apart from them in ideas and cultural
style (though in *From a View to a Death* Powell makes
a similar analysis to Auden of 'a country where no-one
is well'). Graham Greene is a novelist of stature and staying
power who was closest to the central concerns of the Auden
generation, and, as I have shown, admired Auden and
was influenced by him. The mildly surprising discovery
about Greene that I have made in writing this book is
that his pre-war fiction is much more impressive than it

is often given credit for being. By comparison, his later, 'Catholic' novels like *The Power and the Glory* and *The Heart of the Matter* look schematic and unconvincing. Their melodramatic, literary versions of Catholic theology, which always appeared strange and perhaps incredible to secular readers, have now come to seem remote to Catholic readers, in the light of the theological developments that followed the Second Vatican Council. In contrast, Greene's novels of the thirties, which use the conventions of the contemporary thriller and the cinema and are mostly set in England, are full of his own peculiar and stylised form of what Henry James called 'felt life'. They combine a maximum of exact observation with a maximum of individual, even obsessional, response, which I find very satisfying. Such a combination, which I have previously called the intersection of the public and the personal, may not be the only formula for literary achievement. But it does seem to characterise the best and most memorable work of the 1930s.

Notes

INTRODUCTION

1. Graham Hough, *Style and Stylistics* (London, 1969) p. 51.
2. Raymond Williams, 'Literature and Sociology: In Memory of Lucien Goldmann', *New Left Review*, no. 67 (May–June 1971) 3–18.
3. Arnold Rattenbury, 'Total Attainder and the Helots', *Renaissance and Modern Studies*, XX (1976) 103–19.

CHAPTER 1   *Men Among Boys, Boys Among Men*

1. Christopher Isherwood, *Lions and Shadows* (London, 1953) pp. 181–2.
2. Ibid., pp. 77–8.
3. Ibid., p. 172.
4. Ibid., p. 192.
5. Ibid., p. 193.
6. Christopher Isherwood, *Exhumations* (Harmondsworth: Penguin, 1969) p. 209.
7. Christopher Isherwood, *Christopher and His Kind* (London, 1977) p. 197.
8. *Lions and Shadows*, p. 101.
9. Edward Upward, *The Railway Accident and Other Stories* (Harmondsworth: Penguin, 1972) p. 34.
10. John Lehmann, *The Whispering Gallery* (London, 1955) p. 244.
11. *The Railway Accident and Other Stories*, p. 44.
12. Ibid., p. 50.
13. *Lions and Shadows*, p. 274.
14. *In the Thirties* is the first volume of a trilogy, *The Spiral Ascent*, which did not appear in its entirety until 1977.
15. C. Day Lewis, 'The Road These Times Must Take', *Left Review*, I (Nov 1934).
16. Roy Campbell, *Collected Poems*, vol. II (London, 1961) pp. 211–12.
17. Edward Upward, *In the Thirties* (Harmondsworth: Penguin, 1969) p. 108.
18. W. H. Auden in Graham Greene (ed.), *The Old School* (London, 1934) p. 14.
19. Ruthven Todd, *Over the Mountain* (London, 1946) p. 118.

20. C. Day Lewis, 'Letter to a Young Revolutionary', in M. Roberts (ed.), *New Country* (London, 1933) p. 29.
21. Ibid., p. 30.
22. Ibid., p. 36.
23. *The Railway Accident and Other Stories*, p. 227.
24. Philip Toynbee, *Friends Apart* (London, 1954) p. 15.
25. Edgell Rickword, 'Straws for the Wary', *Left Review*, I (Oct 1934) pp. 19–25.
26. John Strachey, 'The Education of a Communist', *Left Review*, I (Dec 1934) pp. 63–9.

CHAPTER 2   *Auden and the Audenesque*

1. Karl Shapiro, *Essay on Rime* (London, 1947) p. 39. The American edition of this work was published in 1945.
2. Ibid., p. 33.
3. A later writer—G. W. Turner, in *Stylistics* (Harmondsworth: Penguin, 1973) p. 85—has made a helpful addition to the discussion:

A whole book, and a very readable and interesting one, *The Tell-Tale Article* by G. Rostrevor Hamilton, has been written on the word *the* in modern poetry. A more technical discussion of the word *the* in Yeats's 'Leda and the Swan' by M. A. K. Halliday can be found in *Patterns of Language* by Angus McIntosh and M. A. K. Halliday. The word *the* is chosen, instead of *a* or a plural without an article, to refer to something known, either universally ('the sun', 'the Bible') or defined within the nominal group ('the point I want to make', 'the King of France', 'the Dover Road', and perhaps long-established London names like 'the Edgware Road') or the general context. When Auden records the mood of left-wing England during the Spanish Civil War, he mentions 'the boring meeting' and 'the flat political pamphlet', where plurals 'boring meetings' and 'flat political pamphlets' would have been the normal choice of earlier poets. Auden's use invites us to think 'Ah, yes, how well we know it all'. Indeed, the frequency of *the* in subsequent poetry, added to its falling intonations, tended towards a universal boredom. We all, like Tiresias, have seen it all. We are not childlike Romantics any more. The crowd of golden daffodils, the rainbow in the sky, the clerk of Oxenford also—none of them are new that way.

4. *Essay on Rime*, p. 41.
5. Ibid., p. 40.
6. Ibid., pp. 40–1.
7. Edward Upward, *The Railway Accident and Other Stories*, p. 83.
8. *Essay on Rime*, p. 40.
9. John Cornford, *Understand the Weapon, Understand the Wound* (Manchester: Carcarnet Press, 1976) pp. 38–40.

10. C. K. Stead, 'Auden's "Spain"', *London Magazine*, VII, no. 12 (Mar 1968) pp. 41–54.
11. Notably by George Orwell in 'Inside the Whale', *Collected Essays, Journalism and Letters*, vol. I (Harmondsworth: Penguin, 1970) pp. 540–78.
12. Julian Symons, *The Thirties: A Dream Revolved* (London, 1960) p. 8.

CHAPTER 3 *Auden/Greene*

1. Graham Greene, *The Pleasure Dome: The Collected Film Criticism 1935–40* (London, 1972) p. 53. Greene's use of 'Audenesque' antedates by four years the first usage recorded in the 1972 Supplement to the *Oxford English Dictionary*.
2. Christopher Isherwood, *The Memorial* (London, 1960) p. 265.
3. Richard Hoggart, *Speaking to Each Other*, vol. II (London, 1970) p. 46.
4. W. H. Auden, 'The Heresy of Our Time', in Samuel Hynes (ed.), *Graham Greene: A Collection of Critical Essays* (Englewood Cliffs, N.J.: Prentice-Hall, 1973) pp. 93–4.
5. This passage from *The End of the Affair* was first set out in this way by Bernard Share, a contributor to the 'Poetry Corner' of *Essays in Criticism* in 1955. I am indebted to Mr Share for helping to launch my present enquiry.

CHAPTER 4 *Transformations of the Frontier*

1. Julian Symons, *The Thirties: A Dream Revolved*, 2nd edition (London, 1975) p. 35.
2. Stephen Spender, *World Within World* (London: Readers Union, 1953) p. 165.
3. Samuel Hynes, *The Auden Generation: Literature and Politics in England in the 1930s* (London, 1976) p. 148.
4. Cyril Connolly, *The Condemned Playground* (London, 1945) p. 180. For the few supporters—in the English-speaking world—of the Nationalist cause, the crossing from France into their zone of Spain was similarly portentous. A graphic account of crossing the frontier from Hendaye to the ruins of Irun is contained in Peter Kemp, *Mine Were of Trouble* (London, 1957) p. 13.
5. Louis MacNeice, *The Strings Are False* (London, 1965) p. 177.
6. Ibid., p. 179.
7. George Orwell, *Homage to Catalonia* (London, 1967) p. 244.
8. Graham Greene, *The Lawless Roads* (Harmondsworth: Penguin, 1971) p. 13.
9. Ibid., pp. 13–14.
10. Ibid., p. 21.
11. Ibid., p. 23.
12. John McCormick in J. Vinson (ed.), *Contemporary Novelists* (London and New York, 1976) p. 1429.
13. *The Auden Generation*, p. 308.
14. The extent to which the idea of the frontier was part of Douglas's

consciousness is nicely illustrated in a letter he wrote in 1938 as a new undergraduate at Oxford, responding to an invitation to tea in Somerville: 'I shall be terrified of venturing within a women's college. Won't I be stopped and interrogated at the frontier?'—Desmond Graham, *Keith Douglas* (London, 1974) pp. 66–7.

CHAPTER 5   *The Last Days of Futurism*

1. F. T. Marinetti in Umbro Apollonio (ed.), *Futurist Manifestos* (London, 1973) p. 21.
2. *Marinetti: Selected Writings* (London, 1972) p. 84.
3. A similar point is made in a recent book published after this chapter was completed: 'These three ['The Landscape Near an Aerodrome', 'The Express' and 'Pylons'], and especially "The Express", may be thought of as some of the few English Futurist poems'—J. A. Morris, *Writers and Politics in Modern Britain* (London, 1977) p. 62. Rupert Brooke in 'The Great Lover', written in 1914, had praised 'the keen / Unpassioned beauty of a great machine'.
4. Antonio Sant'Elia in Apollonio (ed.) *Futurist Manifestos*, p. 169.
5. Alan A. Jackson, *Semi-Detached London* (London, 1973) p. 139.
6. Reyner Banham, 'The Tear-Drop Express', *Times Literary Supplement*, 23 July 1976.
7. Orwell, *Collected Essays, Journalism and Letters*, vol. I, p. 158.
8. Cf. Goodman's later poem 'For Ernst Thaelmann' (in *Left Review*, I, Jan 1935), of which this is an extract:

> Therefore
> with us who soar
> who score
> the sky
> who helmeted ride the air
> veined hand exact
> —oh joystick eager there!—
> declare
> with fuselage and wing
> engine and singing screw
> *bridge space with protest*
> cry
> you and you and you
> here there and everywhere
> *Thaelmann shall not die*

9. Correlli Barnett, *The Collapse of British Power* (London, 1972) p. 436.
10. Shapiro, *Essay on Rime*, p. 39.
11. David Jones, *The Sleeping Lord and Other Fragments* (London, 1974) p. 9.

CHAPTER 6   *Supplying the Lyrics*

1. Douglas Day, *Malcolm Lowry* (London, 1974) pp. 88–9.

2. There is good example in *A Gun for Sale*, where the fugitive killer Raven takes refuge in the garage of a suburban house and overhears a broadcast reading of Tennyson's *Maud*.
3. Philip Stratford, 'Unlocking the Potting Shed', *Kenyon Review*, XXIV (1962) 129–43.
4. Greene, *The Pleasure Dome: The Collected Film Criticism 1935–40*, p. 56.

CHAPTER 7 *Icon or Commodity?*

1. A. J. P. Taylor, *English History 1914–1945* (Oxford, 1965) p. 314.
2. Walter Benjamin, *Illuminations* (London, 1970) pp. 232–3.
3. Greene, *The Pleasure Dome: The Collected Film Criticism 1935–40*, p. 26.
4. T. S. Eliot, 'London Letter', *The Dial*, LXX (June 1921) 686–91.
5. Roland Barthes, *Mythologies* (London, 1972) pp. 56–7.

CHAPTER 8 *Conclusion*

1. George Watson, 'Were the Intellectuals Duped?', *Encounter*, XLI (Dec 1973) 20–30.
2. See the discussion of this question in John Lukacs, *The Last European War*, (London, 1976) pp. 325, 452.
3. Stephen Spender, *World Within World* (London: Readers Union, 1953) p. 183.
4. Christopher Isherwood, *Christopher and His Kind* (London, 1977) pp. 247–8.
5. Tom Wolfe, *The Kandy-Kolored Tangerine-Flake Streamline Baby* (London, 1966) pp. 3–28.
6. Day Lewis, 'Letter to a Young Revolutionary', in Roberts (ed.), *New Country*, p. 40.
7. Orwell, *Collected Essays, Journalism and Letters*, vol. I, p. 548.
8. The Mass Observation movement had a sense of this encounter and tried to examine it. Its founders, Charles Madge and Tom Harrisson, wrote,

> More recent acquisitions to society—electricity, aeroplanes, radio— are so new that the process of adaptation to them is still going on. It is within the scope of the science of Mass Observation to watch the process taking place—perhaps to play some part in determining the adaptation of old superstitions to new conditions.

Quoted in R. Graves and A. Hodge (eds), *The Long Week-End* (London, 1950) p. 402.
9. *Christopher and His Kind*, p. 249.

All the poems by Auden discussed in this book can now be found in *The English Auden*, edited by Edward Mendelson, published late in 1977, after the present work was completed.

Index